W9-CIJ-562

ARCHITECTURE

by Don Nardo

LUCENT BOOKS

An imprint of Thomson Gale, a part of The Thomson Corporation

THOMSON

GALE

720
NAR

Detroit • New York • San Francisco • New Haven, Conn. • Waterville, Maine • London

LIBRARY OF CONGRESS CATALOGING-IN-PUBLICATION DATA

Nardo, Don, 1947–
  Architecture / by Don Nardo.
    p. cm. — (Eye on art)
  Includes bibliographical references and index.
  ISBN-13: 978-1-4205-0003-5 (hardcover)
  1. Architecture—Juvenile literature. I. Title.
  NA2555.N37 2008
  720—dc22

2007022926

ISBN-10: 1-4205-0003-1
Printed in the United States of America

CONTENTS

Foreword

"Art has no other purpose than to brush aside ... everything that veils reality from us in order to bring us face to face with reality itself."
— French philosopher Henri-Louis Bergson

Some thirty-one thousand years ago, early humans painted strikingly sophisticated images of horses, bison, rhinoceroses, bears, and other animals on the walls of a cave in southern France. The meaning of these elaborate pictures is unknown, although some experts speculate that they held ceremonial significance. Regardless of their intended purpose, the Chauvet-Pont-d'Arc cave paintings represent some of the first known expressions of the artistic impulse.

From the Paleolithic era to the present day, human beings have continued to create works of visual art. Artists have developed painting, drawing, sculpture, engraving, and many other techniques to produce visual representations of landscapes, the human form, religious and historical events, and countless other subjects. The artistic impulse also finds expression in glass, jewelry, and new forms inspired by new technology. Indeed, judging by humanity's prolific artistic output throughout history, one must conclude that the compulsion to produce art is an inherent aspect of being human, and the results are among humanity's greatest cultural achievements: masterpieces such as the architectural marvels of ancient Greece, Michelangelo's perfectly rendered statue *David*, Vincent van Gogh's visionary painting *Starry Night*, and endless other treasures.

The creative impulse serves many purposes for society. At its most basic level, art is a form of entertainment or the means for a satisfying or pleasant aesthetic experience. But art's true power lies not in its potential to entertain and delight but in its ability to enlighten, to reveal the truth, and by doing so to uplift the human spirit and transform the human race.

One of the primary functions of art has been to serve religion. For most of Western history, for example, artists were paid by the church to produce works with religious themes and subjects. Art was thus a tool to help human beings transcend mundane, secular reality and achieve spiritual enlightenment. One of the best-known, and largest-scale, examples of Christian religious art is the Sistine Chapel in the Vatican in Rome. In 1508 Pope Julius II commissioned Italian Renaissance artist Michelangelo to paint the chapel's vaulted ceiling, an area of 640 square yards (535 sq. m). Michelangelo spent four years on scaffolding, his neck craned, creating a panoramic fresco of some three hundred human figures. His paintings depict Old Testament prophets and heroes, sibyls of Greek mythology, and nine scenes from the Book of Genesis, including the Creation of Adam, the Fall of Adam and Eve from the Garden of Eden, and the Flood. The ceiling of the Sistine Chapel is considered one of the greatest works of Western art and has inspired the awe of countless Christian pilgrims and other religious seekers. As eighteenth-century German poet and author Johann Wolfgang von Goethe wrote, "Until you have seen this Sistine Chapel, you can have no adequate conception of what man is capable of."

In addition to inspiring religious fervor, art can serve as a force for social change. Artists are among the visionaries of any culture. As such, they often perceive injustice and wrongdoing and confront others by reflecting what they see in their work. One classic example of art as social commentary was created in May 1937, during the brutal Spanish civil war. On May 1 Spanish artist Pablo Picasso learned of the recent attack on the small Basque village of Guernica by German airplanes allied with fascist forces led by Francisco Franco. The German pilots had used the village for target practice, a three-hour bombing that killed sixteen hundred civilians. Picasso, living in Paris, channeled his outrage over the massacre into his painting *Guernica,* a black, white, and gray mural that depicts dismembered animals and fractured human figures whose faces are contorted in agonized expressions. Initially, critics and the public condemned the painting as an incoherent hodgepodge, but the work soon came to be seen as a powerful antiwar statement and remains an iconic symbol of the violence and terror that dominated world events during the remainder of the twentieth century.

The impulse to create art—whether painting animals with crude pigments on a cave wall, sculpting a human form from marble, or commemorating human tragedy in a mural—thus serves many purposes. It offers an entertaining diversion, nourishes the imagination and the spirit, decorates and beautifies the world, and chronicles the age. But underlying all these functions is the desire to reveal that which is obscure—to illuminate, clarify, and perhaps ennoble. As Picasso himself stated, "The purpose of art is washing the dust of daily life off our souls."

The Eye on Art series is intended to assist readers in understanding the various roles of art in society. Each volume offers an in-depth exploration of a major artistic movement, medium, figure, or profession. All books in the series are beautifully illustrated with full-color photographs and diagrams. Riveting narrative, clear technical explanation, informative sidebars, fully documented quotes, a bibliography, and a thorough index all provide excellent starting points for research and discussion. With these features, the Eye on Art series is a useful introduction to the world of art—a world that can offer both insight and inspiration.

Introduction

A Unique Fusion of Science and Art

Architecture has been part of the human experience for many thousands of years. Indeed, to a considerable degree great structures have shaped the image of and made memorable the various stages of human civilization. Some of the more familiar examples include the mighty pyramids of ancient Egypt and central America; the magnificent Parthenon temple of ancient Athens; Notre Dame and other inspiring Gothic cathedrals of medieval Europe; and the towering skyscrapers of modern cities around the world. These examples show that as empires and cultures have risen and fallen over the millennia, architecture, especially monumental (large-scale) architecture, has helped to define their characters.

This close association between great architecture and human cultures is no accident. It arises from some special qualities possessed by architecture. These qualities are intimately connected with human beings, their intellects, their communities, their physical needs, and their emotional and aesthetic (artistic) needs and expression. In sum, architecture is both an inevitable product and distinctive characteristic of human civilization. And as such, it fuses, or brings together, two defining elements of civilized societies. One is science, in the form of technology, essential to structural strength, integrity, and durability. The other is art, in the form of visually and emotionally pleasing forms and decorations. For this reason, effective architecture is frequently said to incorporate "form and function" in more or less equal measures.

Technology Plus Grace

That architecture consists in part of the proper application of science was well known to the ancients. The ancient Egyptians used basic elements of geometry in erecting the huge pyramids at Giza (near modern Cairo), for instance. They also exploited knowledge, gained from experience, about the tensile strength of wood, stone, and other natural materials. (A material's tensile strength is the amount of stress it can endure before breaking.) Later, the Greeks and Romans also employed technology to create monumental architecture and at times acknowledged their need for and debt to science. Writing in the first century B.C., the Roman architect Vitruvius stated:

The ancient Egyptians used geometry in the design and construction of the magnificent pyramids of Giza (pictured).

> The science of the architect depends upon many disciplines. . . . His personal service consists in craftsmanship and technology. Craftsmanship is a continued and

familiar practice, which is carried out by the hands in such material as is necessary for the purpose of a design. Technology sets forth and explains things [made] in accordance with technical skill and method. [1]

Yet Vitruvius, who was supremely educated in the impressive building techniques employed by Rome in his day, did not for a moment view a building merely as a technical, functional commodity. He also recognized the innate human desire for said structure to be pleasing to behold. The best architecture, he contended, should take full account of *"grace,* when the appearance of the work shall be pleasing and elegant, and the scale of the constituent parts is justly calculated by symmetry [visual balance]."[2] Centuries later, the noted Italian Renaissance architect Leon Battista Alberti (1404–1472) also stressed this intrinsic need for artistic elements in architecture, saying:

> There is a certain excellence and natural beauty in the figures and forms of buildings, which immediately strike the mind with pleasure and admiration. It is my opinion that beauty, majesty, gracefulness, and the like charms exist in those particulars which if you alter or take away [those charms], the whole would be made homely [ugly] and disagreeable. [3]

Thus, many great architects of the past held that an effective piece of architecture must possess a balanced mixture of technological and artistic elements. This concept endured into the modern age. True, many modern structures utilize materials more advanced than those available to past cultures; and a number of modern buildings, particularly skyscrapers, look quite different than buildings from past ages. Yet modern architects are just as aware as their predecessors were of the need to appeal to human aesthetic concerns. Today, as in the past, art and science "combine in all buildings," architectural critic James Neal points out. "Without science, buildings are unlikely to have any structural permanence; if they lack art, people would not find them beautiful enough to allow them to remain over the years."[4]

A modern London office building (foreground), nicknamed "The Gherkin," and the Tower of London are examples of two very different styles of architecture.

Living in Three-Dimensional Space

Neal correctly emphasizes the human element, since both technology and art exist to serve people and their needs. Other types of art, such as painting and sculpture, do serve human needs by adorning rooms inside buildings for people's pleasure. And quite often these arts are also used on the outside in architectural decoration. But architecture itself goes beyond the capabilities of other art forms because buildings are places for people to live and work in. Architecture "takes us in," say architectural historians Marvin Trachtenberg and Isabelle Hyman. It "surrounds us, shapes our lives, and protects us."[5]

Because human beings so often dwell within buildings, architecture must create sufficient space to accommodate them and their endeavors. It might be just enough space for a single family to utilize. Or it might be the huge amount of space needed for people to hold public meetings, attend plays and concerts, or watch sporting events.

Either way, architecture itself is sometimes said to "live in," or be physically defined by, three-dimensional space. In the words of architectural historian Anita Abramovitz:

> [Architectural] space, designed and built by human beings, also includes human beings themselves—their comings and goings, their actual *presence*—throughout time and in ever-changing patterns. We ourselves, therefore, are the quality peculiar to architecture, the dimension that distinguishes architecture from all other arts. It is we who call forth the kinds of spaces we need, desire, and enjoy.[6]

Symbols of National Power

Architecture is therefore a tool that fulfills both the functional needs and artistic enjoyment of the people who use it to create their buildings. The community in which those people live often make up a regional or national unit, or even an entire civilization, with its own unique political, economic, intellectual, and artistic aspirations. And a great building or architectural style trumpets the achievements and power of that community or people or civilization. In such cases, says Neal, architecture "is the ultimate mark of confidence in the power and culture of a society, from the great pyramids of Giza to the great palaces and cathedrals of Europe or to their modern equivalents, the museums and municipal buildings of our cities."[7]

In this way, the Parthenon temple was more than a beautiful building paying homage to the goddess Athena. It was also a symbol of the power and glory of ancient Athens, a boast, as well as a warning, to other nations of that time and era. Similarly, today giant skyscrapers advertise the wealth, power, and achievements of those who erect them. And this fact is never lost on the builders' enemies. It was, after all, major architectural symbols of U.S. national power—the World Trade Center towers—that foreign terrorists attacked and destroyed on September 11, 2001.

In the final analysis, then, architecture is a combination of scientific technology and artistic expression that a given people embraces, shapes, and adapts to its own needs and desires. At the same time, great buildings become leading symbols of that people and its accomplishments. Perhaps no one has concisely summed it up better than the late Frank Lloyd Wright, one of the greatest architects of the twentieth century. "The sciences cannot benefit human beings, really," he said, "until creative art takes them up and shows how to use them according to human quality and interests."[8]

The Earliest Civilizations: The Near East and Europe

The size, shape, look, and even the crudest remains of the first human-made structures are forever lost in the mists of time. No one knows for sure what the first artificially constructed building was, who erected it, and where it stood. Still, based on various forms of evidence uncovered in the past century or so from ancient sites across the globe, historians and archaeologists are able to make educated guesses. Most likely, they contend, the first structures were small, meager huts designed to protect people from the weather. These one- or two-room shelters were more or less thrown together using whatever natural materials could be found—branches, logs, straw, packed mud, and so forth.

But can such tiny, rudimentary dwellings qualify as architecture? Most modern architects and architectural historians say no. They generally prefer to view true architecture in terms of monumental, or large-scale, structures built by members of communities to serve their communal needs. The first examples were full-fledged towns and certain large, communal structures (including large defensive walls and religious shrines) in or near those towns.

An important technological key to erecting such imposing monuments was discovered some time in the Neolithic Age, perhaps between 10,000 and 8,000 B.C. (ten to twelve thousand years ago). This was the era in which humans first began practicing agriculture. In fact, historians define Neolithic cultures as those that practiced agriculture but still used stone rather than metal tools and weapons.

Some unknown Neolithic farmer or hunter had the bright idea of the architectural form or unit now called the post and lintel. It consists of two vertical supports, the posts (or pillars or piers), topped by a horizontal beam or slab, the lintel. At first such units were composed of wood. But in time they came to be made of more durable and permanent stone, too. The post and lintel became a crucial component of most large-scale buildings that followed because it allowed people to construct doors and windows in structures and gateways in walls. Most temples, palaces, forts, battlements, and other monumental edifices would have been impossible without this basic architectural concept.

The Earliest Towns and Defensive Walls

Both the beginnings of agriculture and the rise of the first towns and cities took place in the Near East, now called the Middle East. In ancient times the region encompassed what is now Turkey (Anatolia or Asia Minor); what are now Syria, Palestine, and Israel,

The classic post and lintel structure stands out in this nighttime view of Stonehenge.

on the eastern coast of the Mediterranean Sea; Egypt, the northern coast of which also borders the Mediterranean; and lying east of these areas, the mostly flat plains of Mesopotamia, today occupied by Iraq and some surrounding areas.

Among the first if not *the* first Neolithic town in the Near East was an agricultural settlement in southeastern Anatolia. Modern archaeologists dubbed it Çatal Hüyük (chat-al hoo-YUK). It was founded perhaps around 8000 B.C. but reached its greatest size and level of prosperity in the seventh and sixth millennia B.C. Covering some 32 acres (13ha), Çatal Hüyük is certainly the largest known Neolithic site in the Near East. And a number of experts view it as the first clear-cut example of large-scale communal architecture. The town consisted of an imposing-looking monolithic complex of brick houses connected to one another for the sake of mutual security. As Trachtenberg and Hyman describe it:

> The houses were entered through a hole in the roof that was at once chimney and doorway. Movement from house to house took place only over and through the roof. . . . Packed into a continuous cellular structure, the houses presented a solid blank wall to the outside. The defensive compactness and structural economy of this architectural program were successful. Excavations revealed . . . [no] signs that the unusual wealth of the [town] had been plundered.[9]

In the same period in which Çatal Hüyük reached its zenith, farther south in what is now Israel, the Neolithic town of Jericho was erected. Its small houses of mud bricks were not connected, unlike those at Çatal Hüyük. Jericho's mode of defense was instead an even more imposing architectural achievement—a towering defensive wall constructed of stone blocks. Some parts of this wall still reach a height of 12 feet (3.6m). And the structure may have originally stood 20 to 25 feet (6m to 7.5m) high. There was also at least one stone guard tower 30 feet (9m) high. Over time, similar monumental defensive walls were erected all over the Near East.

Mesopotamian Architectural Wonders

Jericho and Çatal Hüyük, each constituting little more than a village by modern standards, were impressive for their time. But from an architectural standpoint, as well as in population, wealth, and power, they paled in comparison with the first cities. These were built in Mesopotamia in the fourth millennium (3000s) B.C. by a people today called the Sumerians. Among the leading Sumerian cities were Ur, Uruk, Lagash, and Nippur, all clustered near the shores of the Persian Gulf. By the start of the third millennium B.C., each of these cities covered several square miles and supported a population in the tens of thousands.

Like Jericho, the Sumerian cities had large-scale defensive walls and battlements for security purposes. But unlike Jericho's stone walls, those surrounding Ur and its neighbors were made of clay bricks. This is because the region of Mesopotamia has very few deposits of natural stone. Some of the bricks featured a mixture of clay and straw or sand, which gave some added strength. People pressed the clay or clay mixture into wooden or pottery molds, then placed the molds outside and allowed the sun to dry them. The city walls constructed of these bricks were nothing less than architectural wonders for their time. Most, like those at Uruk, were at least 6 miles (10km) in circumference, and a few eventually reached nearly twice that size.

The cities of Mesopotamia, both under the Sumerians and later local peoples—including the Babylonians and Assyrians—featured other forms of monumental architecture besides defensive walls. For example, every city in the ancient Near East had one or more structures devoted to religious worship. These communal structures were temples, each dedicated to one or more gods or goddesses.

Some temples were constructed beside or atop enormous pyramid-like structures called ziggurats. A ziggurat was solid (as opposed to Egyptian pyramids, which had interior passageways and chambers) and had one or more large stairways or ramps that priests and kings ascended. These high officials performed various rituals in a small chapel or temple at the top. "In circling up a Babylonian ziggurat," Anita Abramovitz writes, "you would feel yourself above a swampy plain, in a high place where it would not seem so strange to see magic in the stars or to search the heavens for wisdom."[10]

In addition to their heavenly, religious functions, ziggurats had a political dimension. Because of their great size—the one at Ur is some 200 feet (61m) long, 150 feet (45m) wide, and 70 feet (21m) high—they were time-consuming and expensive to erect. This made them symbols of wealth, power, and prestige for those cities that could afford to build them.

Palaces to house local kings and their families were another architectural form the leaders of Mesopotamian cities built to flaunt their wealth and power. A typical palace in the region consisted of several rooms grouped around a central unroofed courtyard. The throne room, meeting halls, and various storage and work facilities were most often located on the ground floor, while one or more upper stories housed the royal bedchambers and other living spaces.

The massive Sumerian ziggurat at Ur (in modern-day Iraq) appears to rise toward the heavens.

Egypt's Timeless Monuments

Not long after the first cities arose on the Mesopotamian plains, cities and religious complexes containing impressive monumental architecture appeared in another pivotal part of the Near East—Egypt. The most famous of these structures are the giant pyramids erected as tombs for Egyptian kings, called pharaohs. Egypt's pyramid-tombs evolved from an earlier, smaller kind of tomb called a mastaba. Rectangular in shape, mastabas were used to inter deceased nobles and, like many structures in Mesopotamia, were composed of clay bricks. Because these bricks disintegrated rapidly, they needed frequent repairs. Also, it was

EGYPTIAN TEMPLES

Besides the famous great pyramids, another form of monumental architecture that has survived in various stages of ruin in Egypt consists of ancient temples. The Egyptians were extremely religiously devout, and they devoted a major portion of their national wealth and energies to building shrines to their gods. They also erected mortuary temples. These were memorials to powerful pharaohs, in which priests prayed and made offerings intended to support the king's spirit in the afterlife.

One of the best preserved ancient Egyptian temples is Medinet Habu in central Egypt, a mortuary temple of King Ramses III (reigned 1184–1153 B.C.). The temple complex begins with two huge pylons, impressive ceremonial gateways common in ancient Egyptian architecture. These lead into an open courtyard. Then come two smaller pylons and a second courtyard, and finally a mammoth hypostyle hall. Another frequent feature of Egyptian architecture, a hypostyle hall is a covered courtyard in which the roof is held up by rows of columns that fill most of the chamber. In the rear of the great hall are a treasury for storing temple valuables and several chapels for prayer and other rituals.

fairly easy for tomb robbers to use stone or metal tools to tunnel through the crumbly walls.

To make the tombs of the nobility more permanent and secure, Egyptian builders increased the size of these structures. They also began fashioning them from stone, which is far more durable and more difficult to penetrate than clay bricks. Then, in the early third millennium B.C. Imhotep, architect to the pharaoh Djoser, conceived a novel idea. He stacked six stone mastabas on top of one another, each slightly smaller than the one below. The result was the world's first pyramid, today called the Step Pyramid. Several other step pyramids were erected in the years that followed. Eventually, builders began filling in the notches of the steps, producing the first smooth-sided, or "true," pyramids.

The most imposing and famous of the pyramids built in Egypt are the three at Giza. The largest, the tomb of the pharaoh Khufu, originally stood 481 feet (147m) high, more than two and a half times taller than New York's Statue of Liberty. The structure measured 756 feet (230m) on each side and covered more than 13

THE IMMORTAL ARCHITECT

The first architect in world history whose name is preserved was Imhotep, who designed the Step Pyramid for the pharaoh Djoser. He also designed a sacred shrine dedicated to Egypt's sun god Ra, a structure now in an advanced state of ruin. Very little is known about Imhotep's life, except that in addition to his work as an architect he served as the pharaoh's seal bearer and vizier (chief administrator). Tradition also credits Imhotep with a great knowledge of medicine. Centuries after his death his reputation as an architect, healer, and wise sage endured, and people began to believe that he had possessed divine qualities. They came to see him as the son of the creator god Ptah and erected several temples in his honor. In this way, Imhotep became, along with the traditional gods and some of the greater pharaohs, one of Egypt's immortals.

acres (5ha) of ground. The other two Giza pyramids—of Khufu's son, Khafre, and Khafre's successor, Menkaure—soared to 478 feet (146m) and 220 feet (67m) respectively.

These and Egypt's few other surviving pyramids are among the oldest examples of great architecture in the world. While many other notable human structures have come and gone, the giants of Giza remain, and they are likely to survive for undetermined ages to come. An Iraqi doctor who visited Egypt about eight hundred years ago, when these monuments were already nearly four thousand years old, aptly remarked: "They stayed continuously against time, and time patiently waits on them."[11]

Europe's Neolithic Builders

During the third millennium B.C., when the peoples of Mesopotamia and Egypt were erecting pyramids, temples, and other imposing architectural wonders, Europe also produced some monumental structures. These have come to be called megalithic. The term comes from the Greek words megas, meaning "great," and lithos, meaning "stone." Accordingly, the megalithic structures are composed of enormous irregular stones, many weighing 10, 20, or 50 tons (9t, 18t, 45t).

Europe's megalithic monuments were built by small localized cultures that existed roughly between 4000 and 1500 B.C. The most notable examples were erected on the Mediterranean islands of Malta, Sardinia, and Sicily, and in Spain, Portugal, France, England, Ireland, and Scotland. Large underground tombs made of immense stones have been found in all of these places. Aboveground megalithic religious temples were also erected. One of the most striking is Hagar Qim, on Malta, built in about 3000 B.C. (or somewhat later). It features six spacious circular rooms and several stone altars, apparently dedicated to a mother goddess associated with fertility.

Hagar Qim, built sometime around 3000 B.C. on the island of Malta, offers a striking example of a megalithic religious temple.

More familiar among Europe's megalithic structures are cromlechs, large circles formed by evenly spaced upright stones. Most famous of all is Stonehenge in southern England, erected in about 2000 B.C. Parts of the monument have fallen over the centuries. But originally it consisted of a series of massive upright stone slabs topped by huge lintel stones that ran around the entire circumference. The purpose of Stonehenge is still debated. Some people have proposed that it was a sort of astronomical observatory; others suggest it was used for religious worship.

Bronze-Age Greece

Although the builders of Europe's megalithic structures were accomplished both technologically and artistically, they did not

A bathroom in the Minoan palace of Knossos features systems for piping in clean water and removing wastes.

MYCENAEAN BURIAL VAULTS

In addition to their monumental palace-citadels, the Mycenaeans built unique stone structures—the *tholos* tombs—to inter their deceased royalty. Archaeologist William R. Biers of the University of Missouri provides this concise description:

> Nowhere is Mycenaean construction seen to better advantage than in the great tholos or beehive tombs of the [Greek] mainland, which were in fact the royal burial vaults associated with the [Mycenaean] palace sites. . . . Tholos tombs were constructed of great blocks of cut stone and have been described as stonelined holes. A deep circular cut in a hillside was lined with blocks laid in a corbel style [having each successive block slightly overhang the one below], so that the diameter of the circle decreased until the final opening at the top could be closed with a capstone.

William R. Biers, *The Archaeology of Greece*. Ithaca, NY: Cornell University Press, 1996, pp. 74, 76.

build a civilization in the classic sense. That is, they did not have cities, nations, forms of writing, and mastery of metallurgy, as the Egyptians and Mesopotamians did. Europe's first true civilization in this sense was that of the Minoans. A non-Greek-speaking people, they inhabited the large Greek island of Crete and other nearby islands in the Aegean Sea in the third and second millennia B.C. This was during Greece's Bronze Age, when people used tools and weapons made of bronze, an alloy of copper and tin.

Chief among Minoan contributions to monumental architecture were several enormous, complex palace-centers. Each covered many acres and featured asymmetrical, multistoried, often split-level clusters of rooms, all arranged around a spacious central courtyard. One of the more vivid recent general descriptions of a Minoan palace is by Dartmouth College scholar Jeremy B. Rutter: "The architecture of the palace is arranged in an irregularly stepped series of projecting rectangular masses resembling a compactly arranged pile of cardboard boxes of different sizes."[12] Among other refinements, the Minoan palaces had advanced plumbing and drainage systems that both piped in clean water and removed wastes.

The purpose of these structures was not simply to provide luxurious accommodations for Minoan leaders. The palace-centers were also the proud focus of community life and activities, including religious worship and sporting events. The central courtyard, archaeologist William R. Biers points out, "may have served as the site of processions, religious rituals, and other ceremonial functions and perhaps of the bull games [in which young men and women leaped over the backs of giant bulls] that we know from artistic representations."[13]

The Minoans exerted considerable cultural influence over the first Greek speakers in the region—the Mycenaeans, who dwelled on the Greek mainland. The Mycenaeans erected some imposing palace-citadels made of giant irregular stones similar to those used by Europe's megalithic builders. These structures, along with the Cretan palace-centers, were abandoned when the Minoan-Mycenaean civilization fell in about 1200 B.C. The region of Greece then entered a long cultural dark age. Several centuries would pass before a new civilization would arise there, one whose unique new architectural forms would have a profound influence on world architecture ever after.

The Earliest Civilizations: Asia and Mesoamerica

A lthough the world's first cities appeared in Mesopotamia in the fourth millennium B.C., other parts of the world were not far behind. In the centuries that followed, cities, and eventually nations and empires, arose in the vast region sometimes referred to as the Far East. Encompassing mainly central and eastern Asia, it included India, China, Japan, and what are now Cambodia, Thailand, Vietnam, and their close neighbors. All of these lands developed communal and monumental architecture, some of it no less massive and impressive than that produced in Mesopotamia, Egypt, and Minoan Crete.

On the whole, architectural styles in the Far East were, structurally and visually speaking, considerably different from those that subsequently developed in the West (Europe and the regions surrounding it). Another major difference between West and East was the phenomenon of architectural evolution. Western styles tended to change significantly over time, while Eastern ones, after attaining an initial level of development, remained more or less the same. "Instead of a series of styles and trends," Neal points out,

the architecture of Eastern civilizations remained static for many centuries, much as that of the ancient

Egyptians. . . . [Partly because of] their strong philosophical religions, there was no need for the usual Western diversity of styles. The East developed a style that fitted its divine requirements and felt no need to diverge from this path.[14]

But despite these differences, the ancient civilizations of the East and West shared one basic and pivotal architectural theme: Namely, the central focus of their monumental architecture was the religious temple or shrine. As in early Egypt, Malta, Sumeria, and Babylonia, large, often elaborate temples sprang up all over the Far East.

Temples dedicated to the gods were also the primary focus of large-scale architecture in Mesoamerica. This is a general term given by modern scholars to the area and early civilizations of Central America—especially what is now southern Mexico. Here, in the first millennium B.C. and first millennium A.D., several

Religion figured prominently in both Eastern and Western architecture. Pictured is the Shimogamo Shrine, rebuilt in the eleventh century in Kyoto, Japan.

culturally advanced peoples arose, including the Olmec, Zapotec, Teotihuacáno, and Maya.

These peoples developed an architectural style that was, on the whole, as different from the Western and Far Eastern traditions as the latter two were from each other. Yet again, certain basic themes were similar in all three traditions. First, as in the ancient West and Far East, the central focus of monumental architecture in Mesoamerica was the religious temple. Also, all three regions utilized the idea of a sacred mound or cosmic hemisphere (dome) having some kind of divine meaning. In Mesopotamia, the ziggurat represented the sacred mound of creation, for instance, as did the pyramidal form in Egypt. And the Mesoamericans also erected pyramids (though stylistically different from those in Egypt) having religious significance.

The Buddhist Stupa

The Far Eastern equivalent of ziggurats and pyramids was the stupa. The basic form of the stupa originated somewhere in southern Asia perhaps in the early first millennium B.C. or earlier. At first stupas were burial mounds, the largest used to inter royalty. In fact, the word *stupa* means "piled up," reflecting that people heaped up a large quantity of earth to make one. But over time stupas became more architecturally sturdy and elaborate and took on cosmic meaning. Fired bricks or stone blocks were stacked around the hemispheric mound and sometimes these were plastered and painted. Also, circular walls, fences, or other enclosures were erected around stupas, which came to represent the cosmos, or abode of the divine.

Such architectural advances in stupas and their increased use in religious rituals coincided with the coming of Buddhism to southern Asia. That important new faith was based on the life experiences and ideas of an Indian prince named Siddhartha, born in about 563 B.C. After having a spiritual awakening, in which he supposedly attained true wisdom, he became known as the Buddha, or "enlightened one." Those who subsequently followed his philosophy believed (and still believe) that it allowed them to attain spiritual peace and to better control their own lives and fate.

India's dome-shaped Great Stupa, located at Sanchi, is a symbol of enlightenment.

Following the Buddha's death, Buddhism spread swiftly to neighboring lands, including China, Thailand, Cambodia, Korea, and eventually Japan. And the new faith exerted a tremendous influence on the development of Far Eastern architecture. Stupas, for example, were transformed into shrines that symbolically linked Buddha's remains and enlightened ideas to the cosmos. Buddhist stupas were constructed by the thousands across southeast Asia and became a dominant trademark of the faith.

Among the more outstanding examples is the so-called Mahastupa, or Great Stupa, at Sanchi, in north-central India. It is an impressive 120 feet (37m) across and 54 feet (15.5m) high. University of Washington scholar Francis D.K. Ching describes it as "a solid mass built up in the form of hundreds of stone rings [each composed of individual stone blocks] that were surfaced with plaster and painted."[15] The Mahastupa is surrounded by a stone balustrade (a system of posts topped by a railing) called a *vedka*. Smaller *vedkas* rim both the lower portion and top of the great dome.

Buddhist and Hindu Temples

Early Buddhist stupas like the Mahastupa at Sanchi had a profound influence on most of the Far Eastern cultures that followed.

These structures became architectural models that were copied, with some variations and refinements, again and again far and wide. First, the basic design elements of Buddhist stupas can be seen in Buddhist temples across southeast Asia. One of the largest and most beautiful examples is the Shwezigon Pagoda, completed in Burma (now called Myanmar, situated west of Thailand) in 1102 A.D. A pagoda is a tower consisting of several separate tiers stacked atop one another. In some areas it became customary to stack a stupa on top of a series of decorated tiers (or levels), producing a pagoda. Thus, the Shwezigon structure's stupa, sheathed in gold, sits atop five elaborately decorated square-shaped tiers, each featuring an outer walkway. "A steep flight of steps at the center of [each] of the four sides of the stepped base gives [religious] pilgrims access to the [walkways],"[16] Ching explains. The entire temple is 160 feet (49m) high and the same distance across at the base.

The stupa form also served as a basis for many of the Hindu temples in India. An early form of Hinduism, the Vedic faith, arose in India several centuries before Buddhism did. (Siddhartha

MASSES OF DIVINE SCULPTURES

The Rajasimhesvara Temple, built between A.D. 700 and 750 at Kanchipuram in southern India, displays the use of masses of divine sculptures that became typical in Hindu shrines. The temple proper is surrounded by a rectangular stone wall. All along the inside surface of this wall the builders placed niches containing minor shrines celebrating various aspects of the goddess Shiva, each shrine featuring statues and frescoes (paintings done on wet plaster). The outside walls of the temple itself also bear numerous intricately carved gods. And similar carvings adorn the temple's massive *shikhara*, a pagoda-like tower seen in nearly every Hindu temple.

himself was born a Vedic Hindu.) After Buddhism spread from India to other lands, Vedic worshippers steadily absorbed its ideals and eventually deified Buddha, making him an incarnation, or earthly form, of their great god Vishnu, the preserver. One result of the merging of the two faiths (along with some other cultural influences) was a more mature form of Hinduism similar to that practiced today. (Another result was that eventually Buddhism as a distinct faith largely disappeared from India.)

The Hindu gods are prominent architectural elements in Hindu temples. Besides Vishnu and his incarnation Buddha, other leading Hindu deities include Brahma, the creator; Shiva, the destroyer; and the elephant-headed Ganesh. Crowded groups of statues and carved reliefs of these and other Hindu gods became standard decorations on the outsides and insides of Hindu temples. Worshippers viewed them as divine guardians. Most Hindu temples also came to feature *shikharas*, pagoda-like towers that were essentially vertical extensions of the stupa form.

The glistening gold top and multitiered tower of the Shwezigon Pagoda in Myanmar offer a striking example of a southeast Asian Buddhist temple.

JAPANESE PAGODAS

Shortly after the building of the Songyue Temple in northeastern China in the sixth century, Buddhism arrived in Japan. And in the centuries that followed the Japanese erected hundreds of temples featuring pagodas. The five-tiered pagoda gracing the Horyu-ji Temple at Nara, Japan, illustrates the architectural distinction between Japanese pagodas and most of those on the Asian mainland. In the Japanese version (strongly influenced by Korean Buddhist architectural elements), the eaves, or roof edges, of each tier extend several feet outward from the building's central core; also, the ends of the eaves curve upward slightly, giving the whole structure an uplifting, graceful appearance.

In fact, Hindu *shikharas* became the model for the pagodas that steadily rose across China and Japan when Buddhism spread through these lands. The oldest surviving Buddhist pagoda in China is part of the Songyue Temple at Dengfeng in northeastern China, erected in the sixth century. The pagoda has twelve sides, stands 131 feet (40m) high, and has fifteen stacked tiers.

The Zenith of Eastern Architecture

Most of the Buddhist and Hindu temples and shrines erected across Asia and Japan in the seventeen centuries following the Buddha's death were no less visually beautiful and impressive than the Shwezigon and Songyue temples. But none compare in sheer size and splendor with Angkor Wat, originally a Hindu temple at Angkor, Cambodia. It was built in the twelfth century by

The size and splendor of Angkor Wat, built in the twelfth century in what is now Cambodia, are unrivaled in ancient architecture.

Suryavarman II, a king of the powerful Khmer Empire (which encompassed a large portion of southeast Asia from about 800 to 1430). The structure was dedicated to Vishnu, as revealed by its native name—Vrah Visnulok, meaning "Vishnu's Abode." The name Angkor Wat was coined later by Europeans.

Among the first European visitors to Angkor Wat was a Portuguese monk who saw it in 1586. "[It] is of such extraordinary construction that it is not possible to describe it with a pen," he said, "particularly since it is like no other building in the world. It has towers and decoration and all the refinements which the human genius can conceive of."[17] A later French traveler was equally impressed, remarking that the temple rivaled the greatest architectural works of ancient Greece and Rome. This assessment is no exaggeration. Angkor Wat covers an immense area measuring 3,378 by 2,690 feet (1,030m by 820m) and features five huge *shikharas*, the tallest of which is 141 feet

(43m) high. In addition, the temple walls contain tens of thousands of square feet of relief sculptures depicting the exploits of Hindu gods and heroes.

Angkor Wat is among a few structures that, for sheer size and scope, marked the zenith of Far Eastern architecture. Another is the world famous Great Wall of China. An English lord who saw it in 1793 declared: "It is certainly the most stupendous work of human hands, for I imagine that if the outline of all the masonry of all the forts and fortified places in the whole world were to be calculated, it would fall considerably short of that of the Great Wall of China."[18]

Actually the Great Wall is not a single structure but a collection of several different walls. They were erected in fits and starts by different Chinese rulers over a span of some eighteen hundred years, beginning in the third century B.C., mainly to discourage raids by enemy tribes living north and northwest of China. Their combined length is about 6,214 miles (10,000km). And almost thirty thousand guard towers and signal towers have survived. (A watchman lit a fire to warn of enemy raiders and watchmen in nearby towers passed the warning along by lighting their own fires.)

It is easy to see why these amazing monumental constructions were such effective defenses. Large portions of the surviving walls are about 20 feet (6m) thick and up to 28.5 feet (8.7m) high. At first, most of the walls were made of rammed earth, clay and sand mixed with water and highly compacted to form building blocks. Later sections of the wall utilized stronger brick and stone construction.

Mesoamerican Pyramids

Though the Mesoamericans never produced architecture on the scale of the Great Wall of China, they did erect several monumental structures no less impressive than Angkor Wat and Egypt's giant pyramids. The first advanced civilizations in Mesoamerica arose in the early first millennium B.C. Apparently much early worship there occurred on hilltops. Over time it became customary to create large earthen mounds as substitutes for sacred hilltops; and in turn, these mounds developed into a true architectural form—pyramids.

In some ways the American pyramids resemble Mesopotamian ziggurats and Egypt's Step Pyramid. All three versions consist of several stepped levels, each smaller than the ones below it. However, the American pyramids are different than their Near Eastern counterparts in some key ways. First, each level of the Step Pyramid rises at nearly a right angle to the top of the level below it. In contrast, succeeding levels in Mesoamerican pyramids slope inward at a distinct angle, producing a more stream-lined look. Also, the American pyramids were constructed differently than pyramids in other lands. The pyramids at Giza were great masses of piled stones; the ziggurat at Ur was a huge pile of sun-dried bricks. Most Mesoamerican pyramids, however,

The Pyramid of the Sun rises above the once-vibrant city of Teotihuacán in Mexico's central highlands.

consisted of a network of stone walls contained within an outer stone wall, with earth and rubble packed into the spaces between the walls.

One of the largest and the most architecturally influential of the Mesoamerican pyramids is the Pyramid of the Sun. Still in a remarkably fine state of preservation, it stands in the midst of a gigantic ceremonial center at Teotihuacán in Mexico's central highlands. The city of Teotihuacán, of which the ceremonial center was the heart, was built in the late first millennium B.C. and early first millennium A.D. It covered an estimated 8 square miles (20 sq. km) and supported a population of more than 150,000. The Pyramid of the Sun consists of six stepped levels rising from a square base. Each side of the base is 739 feet (226m) long (only slightly less than the sides of Khufu's pyramid at Giza), and the structure rises to a height of just over 200 feet (60m). People accessed the summit via a grand staircase located in the front.

The Pyramid of the Sun exerted a strong influence on later Mesoamerican peoples, including the Toltec, Maya, and Aztec. Its features were reproduced "in countless variations of size, shape, and proportion throughout central Mexico," says architectural historian Frederick Hartt. "Its form became sharply steeper and higher in the Mayan civilization."[19] These great brick and stone pyramids demonstrate that Mesoamerican architecture was at least as large-scale and ambitious as that created in Europe in the same age.

The Classical Tradition: Ancient Greece and Rome

I n the late second and early first millennia B.C., as Hinduism was forming in the Far East, Europe seemed to hold little promise of becoming a wellspring of great architecture. The cultures of the megalithic builders had disappeared by this time. And with the fall of the Minoan-Mycenaean civilization circa 1200 B.C., the mighty palaces of the Bronze Age Greeks lay abandoned and falling into ruin.

For roughly three centuries the Greeks languished in a cultural dark age. Like people in other parts of Europe at the time, they lived in small impoverished villages, each more or less isolated from its neighbors in a valley or on an island. No monumental architecture was produced nor even envisioned.

Yet, as time passed a new civilization began to emerge in the Greek region, one more vibrant, innovative, and influential than any before seen in Europe. In an era that historians call the Archaic Age (ca. 800–500 B.C.), that new culture steadily attained economic prosperity. There was also widespread political experimentation in the Greek lands. Hundreds of city-states, each viewing itself as a small, independent nation, arose. And at the start of the next era (as determined by modern historians), the Classical Age (ca. 500–323 B.C.), the most populous city-state, Athens, introduced the world's first democracy.

The Greeks also introduced new artistic styles, including a unique form of architecture initially conceived for religious temples. In the late Archaic Age and early Classical Age, magnificent stone temples sprang up in Greece and in Greek cities that had recently been established across the Mediterranean world. In addition, the Greeks designed and built the world's first theaters.

All through these years Greek culture, including architectural styles and elements, entranced and profoundly influenced other European peoples. In particular, the Romans, whose culture arose in Italy in the early first millennium B.C., absorbed the basics of Greek architecture. While the Greeks were artistic innovators, the Romans were brilliant imitators. The Romans were also more visionary and ambitious engineers than the Greeks. As a result, Roman civilization applied architectural ideas borrowed from the Greeks in ways that suited Rome's individual needs and did so on a scale vaster than the world had yet seen. Another pivotal Roman achievement was to preserve Greece's artistic legacy and pass it on to later Europeans, who in turn gave it to the world. The Greco-Roman, or classical, tradition was destined to become the strongest single force in later world architecture.

Dwelling Places for the Gods

The reason that classical Greek architecture developed around the needs of the temple was that the Greeks, like the Egyptians, were religiously devout. During the dark age a common religion spread across the Greek lands with a pantheon (group) of gods headed by Zeus, whose chief symbol was the thunderbolt. But though all Greeks worshipped the same gods overall, each city-state had its own patron deity. The patron of Athens, for instance, was Athena, goddess of war and wisdom. It was thought that Athena protected and frequently visited the community and therefore required a place to stay there. For this reason, temples were the

Throughout ancient Greece, architects oversaw construction of exquisite temples and other structures, as depicted in this illustration.

first form of monumental architecture that developed in post-dark-age Greece. The Greeks lavished huge amounts of time, money, and energy in making temples as aesthetically pleasing as possible. The temple was seen as an ideal architectural form because it honored and served the gods. "The philosophy behind Greek architecture," Neal points out,

> was to discover the eternally valid rules that dictate form and proportion; to construct buildings of human scale that were suited to the divinity of their gods. Classical Greek architecture is [therefore] "ideal architecture." [It is no wonder] that elements of the style have been copied for over 2,500 years. [20]

The earliest Greek temples were small, simple, hut-like structures made mostly of wood. They featured a front porch with a triangular pediment (the gable formed by the slanted roof), supported by two or four thin wooden columns. As the Archaic Age progressed, these structures rapidly increased in size, complexity, and splendor. Builders added more columns, eventually forming a full colonnade (row of columns) that stretched around the whole building. The first known temple in this style was erected on the Aegean island of Samos in the early 700s B.C. Dedicated to Hera, Zeus's divine wife, it was about 106 feet (32m) long, 21 feet (6m) wide, and had a colonnade featuring forty-three wooden columns. A more or less standard temple design now emerged. It featured a rectangular inner enclosure with a main room called a *cella*; a front and back porch, each with a row of columns; colonnades running down the sides; and a low-pitched roof forming a triangular pediment on each end.

These basic architectural elements remained more or less the same for ages to come. However, the materials used in constructing temples became stronger and more durable over time. The roofs, for example, were originally composed of wooden timbers and thatch (thickly intertwined tree branches). In late Archaic times, pottery roofing tiles replaced the wood and thatch. And because the tiles were very heavy, it became necessary to replace the wooden columns supporting the roof with stronger stone versions. By the dawn of the Classical Age, the changeover to all-stone temples was complete almost everywhere in Greece.

Architectural Orders and the Parthenon

The late Archaic Age also witnessed the widespread adoption of two styles of architectural decoration, called orders. Temples on the Greek mainland primarily utilized the Doric order. Their columns stood directly on the temple floor without any sort of decorative base, and the column tops, or capitals, consisted of a rounded stone cushion resting under a flat stone slab. Doric buildings also featured a frieze, a decorative painted or sculpted band running horizontally above the colonnade. Doric friezes were not continuous but were divided into separate rectangular elements, or panels, called metopes.

Meanwhile, the other popular architectural order, the Ionic, became dominant in the Aegean islands and in western Anatolia, then a Greek region known as Ionia. Ionic columns had decorative bases. Also, their capitals featured elegant carved spirals called volutes. Another distinctive aspect of the Ionic style was the nature of its frieze. Rather than a series of separate panels, the frieze formed a continuous band above the colonnade. (A third Greek order, the Corinthian, developed much later and was exploited more by the Romans than the Greeks. The capitals of Corinthian columns were ornately decorated with carved leaves and scrolls.)

On occasion Greek architects mixed various elements of the Doric and Ionic orders. An outstanding example is the Parthenon, a temple of Athena erected atop Athens's central hill, the Acropolis, in the fifth century B.C. It featured two friezes.

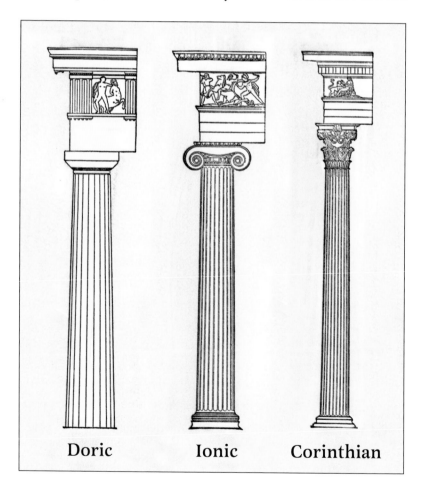

Doric, Ionic, and Corinthian columns represent three classical styles of architectural decoration.

Doric   **Ionic**   **Corinthian**

THE ATYPICAL ERECHTHEUM

Resting near the remains of the Parthenon on Athens's Acropolis are the ruins of another temple dedicated to Athena—the Erechtheum (or Erechtheion). In a popular ancient myth, that goddess tossed an olive-wood statue of herself onto the Acropolis and the early Athenians built the first version of the Erechtheum on the spot where the statue landed. The version whose remains now exist was erected centuries later during the vast building program overseen by the famous politician Pericles in the late fifth century B.C. Architecturally speaking, the Erechtheum followed a plan that was quite unusual for Greek temples of that time. It had four porches, one each on its north, south, east, and west sides, all set in an asymmetrical, split-level arrangement. The south-facing porch came to be called the "Porch of the Maidens" because its roof is supported by six kary-atids, pillars shaped like maidens wearing flowing robes. (The karyatids standing there today are exact replicas, as the originals now reside in the safety of various museums.)

A standard outward-facing Doric frieze graced the area above the colonnade. Meanwhile, a magnificent Ionic frieze containing hundreds of sculptured human and animal figures ran around the perimeter on the inside of the colonnade. The reason for this extra and expensive decoration was that the Parthenon's designers, the architect Ictinus and sculptor Phidias, conceived it on a grander scale than most other Greek temples. It originally contained 22,000 tons (19,800t) of marble and its roof weighed an estimated 3,000 tons (2,700t). The peaks of its pediments soared 65 feet (20m)—nearly seven stories—above the ground. And splendid larger-than-life-sized sculpted figures of people and gods filled the open spaces within the pediments. The Parthenon has

inspired awe in all who have seen it throughout the ages, and many modern architects call it the most perfect building ever created. One nineteenth-century visitor to Athens remarked: "All the world's culture culminated in Greece, all Greece in Athens, all Athens in its Acropolis, all the Acropolis in the Parthenon."[21]

Other Greek Buildings

The Greeks applied elements of temple architecture, including the Doric and Ionic orders, to other public buildings. Among these were treasuries, small ornately decorated structures for storing gold and other valuables. In fact, Greek treasuries looked very much like miniature versions of temples. Greek fountain houses, small buildings that held supplies of fresh water, also looked like miniature temples. In addition, every Greek city-state had one or more town hall–like structures where local officials met and public banquets were staged. Such buildings were usually square-shaped, with rows of Doric or Ionic columns both outside and inside.

Still another public structure common to Greek cities in the Classical Age and for centuries afterward was the theater. The Athenians invented both written plays and the institution of the theater in the late 500s B.C. Not long afterward, the Athenians constructed the Theater of Dionysus, situated at the foot of the Acropolis. It consisted of a circular orchestra, or "dancing place," where the actors performed, and a semicircular audience area that eventually sat up to fourteen thousand people. A rectangular structure called the *skene*, or "scene building," was erected behind the orchestra. The *skene* provided a background for the actors and also housed dressing rooms and perhaps a storage area for stage props.

GREEK STOAS

*A*lthough religious temples were the most splendid examples of monumental architecture in ancient Greece, the Greeks did produce some large-scale secular architecture, too. One of the most common and visually beautiful examples was the stoa. Erected most often in marketplaces, like the agora in Athens, it was a long rectangular structure with an open walkway running along the front. The overhanging roof of the walkway was supported by a graceful row of Doric or Ionic columns. And to the rear of this open-air corridor were several small chambers used variously as workrooms and merchants' stalls. The roofed walkways of stoas were a place for people to find shelter from the sun and rain. Over time they also became meeting places, where informal political and philosophical discussions and educational lectures took place. (A famous group of philosophers, the Stoics, were named for the stoa.) One stoa in the Athenian agora was called the Stoa Poikile, or "Painted Stoa." It earned this name because it contained several large painted murals.

Roman Practicality and Grandeur

In a number of ways Roman architecture, especially that of temples, looked similar to Greek architecture. This is not surprising, since the Romans borrowed outright most of the design elements of Greek temple architecture. But there were significant differences between the architectural traditions and achievements of the two peoples. If Greek architecture can be summed up by words such as "beautiful" and "innovative," the key words describing Roman architecture are "practical" and "grand." Over the course of several centuries the Romans created a huge empire with a largely efficient centralized government, a feat the Greeks never managed. And the needs of empire demanded some new kinds of public structures that were both practical and large scale. "The complexities and importance of large-scale commerce," one expert observer notes,

> called for open, large-scale interior spaces that could be enlivened by the hustle and bustle of much human traffic and activity. Law courts needed impressive, high-ceilinged chambers. Extensive, many-chambered, roofed-over spaces were needed for . . . such popular diversions as the public baths. Vast amphitheaters and arenas were needed for entertaining the tax-paying populace. [22]

The Roman amphitheaters were huge oval-shaped stadiums for staging gladiatorial combats and wild animal shows. The biggest and most famous was the Colosseum in Rome. In its heyday the structure's oval bowl measured 620 by 513 feet (189m by 157m) in breadth and over 156 feet (47m) in height. The seats are no longer intact, so the exact seating capacity is uncertain. But the consensus of modern experts is that the Colosseum held some fifty thousand spectators.

Even larger than amphitheaters were facilities called circuses, where the Romans held chariot races. In each circus huge stone seating sections surrounded a dirt racetrack with a long, narrow barrier, the *euripus*, running down the middle. The *euripus* was crowded with statues, altars, pillars, and other decorative elements. And in each race the charioteers drove their teams seven times around the *euripus*, a distance of roughly 3 miles (4.8km). The largest and most famous Roman circus was the Circus Maximus in Rome. A true wonder of the world, it was some 2,040 feet (622m) long, 450 feet (137m) wide, and sat at least 150,000 people.

In addition to large-scale facilities for entertainment, the Romans also erected basilicas—huge public structures used for political meetings, law courts, and various administrative and social functions. Architecturally speaking, a basilica consisted of a large open central space, called the nave, with spacious aisles running down its sides. High above the nave loomed a vaulted

Visitors to Rome flock to the huge oval-shaped Colosseum, which once held gladiatorial combats and wild animal shows.

FAME FROM A BOOK, NOT A BUILDING

In medieval and modern times, the best-known ancient Roman architect was Marcus Vitruvius Pollio, most often referred to simply as Vitruvius. In reality, he was not one of Rome's greater architects. Rather, his later fame rested mainly on his penning, in the 20s B.C., of a treatise titled *De Architectura,* Latin for *On Architecture.* The work covers all kinds of Greek and Roman building, along with related topics including common building materials, mathematics, civil engineering, town planning, the architectural orders, aqueducts, mechanical devices, and more. After Rome's fall, a few handwritten copies of the book survived. And in 1486 the first published edition became a sensation among European architects and intellectuals. Very little is known about Vitruvius's life beyond the fact that he was a practicing Roman architect and engineer from about 46 to 30 B.C.

roof. And outside each entrance was a covered porch lined with columns. Basilicas turned out to be one of the most important Roman contributions to world architecture, because over time their form became the basis for many early Christian churches.

Roman Trademarks

Basilicas, amphitheaters, and most other Roman architectural forms consistently utilized certain architectural elements and construction materials that became Roman trademarks. Among the more familiar are the arch and vault. A Roman arch featured two vertical stone piers topped by a semicircle composed of wedge-shaped stones called voussoirs (voo-SWARS). The central and topmost voussoir was called the keystone. A Roman vault was essentially an arch carried into three dimensions—a curved ceiling.

St. Peter's Basilica in Rome incorporates Roman architectural elements including the arch and vault system (right and left) and a barrel vault (top).

If such a ceiling ran down the length of the corridor, it was called a barrel vault, a common feature of the corridors of both theaters and amphitheaters in Roman lands.

Another trademark of Roman building was the use of concrete in addition to marble, granite, wood, and other traditional materials. In the third century B.C. the Romans found that adding a special kind of volcanic sand to lime in a specific ratio produced a remarkably hard, strong, and durable substance. Another advantage was that Roman concrete hardened underwater, making it ideal for building bridges over rivers. Constituting another of Rome's great achievements in monumental architecture, some of these bridges were so sturdy that they are still in use and easily carry the weight of cars and trucks.

Moreover, just as Roman bridges survived the centuries to be used, reused, and endlessly copied; and as basilicas evolved into churches; so too did the Greco-Roman architectural tradition as a whole outlive the ancient civilizations that created it. Its ideas would later be incorporated into the facades of thousands of diverse structures erected across the globe. Roman architecture absorbed and enlarged upon Greek architecture, the great art historian Mortimer Wheeler wrote. And this set the stage for "that astonishing afterlife in which [the Greco-Roman tradition] was to dominate the post-Renaissance world down to the noonday of modern times."[23]

Castles and Cathedrals: The Medieval Era

I n the era following the fall of the Roman Empire in the fifth and sixth centuries, existing architectural styles in most parts of the world did not change much. In the Far East, for example, builders continued to use variations of the Buddhist stupa for temples and shrines; and Mesoamerican builders perpetuated the pyramid and other architectural forms displayed so brilliantly at Teotihuacán in the early first millennium.

In contrast, architecture in Europe was far less static. Its medieval era witnessed not only widespread construction of large-scale buildings but also a steady evolution of architectural styles. (Historians view Europe's medieval era as the period that separated ancient times from modern times and date it from about A.D. 500 to 1500 or 1600.) Two principal categories of architecture developed in medieval Europe—secular (nonreligious) and religious. Most of the secular architecture was defensive in nature and revolved around castles. The religious architecture consisted of thousands of churches and cathedrals erected across the continent, some of them enormous. These structures underwent a progression of stylistic changes and innovations that would eventually culminate in Europe's Renaissance. Meanwhile, along the eastern and southern fringes of medieval Europe, another distinct style of architecture—Islamic—was developing.

Castles for Control and Defense

Along with churches, castles were the architectural trademarks, so to speak, of medieval Europe. Not only architecturally, but also militarily and socially, castles dominated the lives of medieval Europeans, especially after the year 1000. Castles housed the continent's kings, lords, and other nobles. And these structures became the main local and regional centers of food distribution, tax collection, political and legal decision making, and warfare. In these ways, the masters of castles exerted control over the thousands of ordinary people who dwelled in surrounding farms and villages.

The basic architectural concepts that went into the creation of the first castles in Europe were not new. Large fortresses had been common in the Near East for thousands of years. And the ancient Romans had erected massive forts across many parts of Europe.

Medieval European builders began erecting primitive castles in northern France in the late ninth and early tenth centuries, and the idea rapidly spread to Germany and other neighboring lands. Made primarily of wood, these structures became known as "motte and bailey" castles. A motte was a low hill on which the builders constructed a wooden stockade. Below the motte and also protected by a stockade were one or more baileys, spacious courtyards in which people as well as domestic animals could find protection when enemies threatened.

A new and larger phase of castle-building began in the eleventh century. Steadily, the older wooden enclosures were replaced with sturdier, more durable stone walls. The result was a structure called a shell keep. It consisted of a circular stone wall encasing a wide courtyard, which contained workshops, stables, and small living quarters. The tops of the walls featured an idea borrowed from ancient Near Eastern fortresses—crenellation. It consisted of alternating stone notches and open spaces; during an attack soldiers hid behind the notches and fired arrows through the open spaces. Simple shell keeps quickly developed into larger, more complex structures with taller, thicker walls and stone living quarters in the centers of the courtyards. The largest single room was usually called the "hall" and served as both a reception and meeting area and a dining room for the castle's residents.

Meanwhile, weapons technology was advancing, making sieges of castles more successful. In response, the outer defenses—or battlements—of European castles became increasingly more formidable. "It was the serious affair of every great leader," the late historian Sidney Toy wrote, "to be familiar with the latest methods of attack and defense, since his safety and the safety of his followers depended on his ability to [repel an] assault."[24] To this end, builders added such features as tall, crenellated guard towers, machicolation, and the portcullis. Machicolation consisted of the outward projection of a wall at the top of the battlements. Missiles or boiling oil could be dropped onto attackers through openings in the floors of these projections. A portcullis was a heavy gateway door constructed of thick wood reinforced

The ancient Romans built many forts in Europe, including this one which has been preserved in northern England.

Chepstow Castle, in Wales, has a crenellated guard tower that became a typical feature of eleventh-century European castles.

with iron plates. Defenders could move it up and down using chains attached to a winch operated from a small chamber above the main gate.

Many European castles also had a drawbridge in front of the portcullis. A drawbridge was a wooden platform that usually rested in a horizontal position over the protective moat (wide pit) surrounding most castles. During an attack the defenders pulled the drawbridge upward, using chains attached to the outer ends of the bridge, until the bridge stood upright against the front of the portcullis.

One of the most imposing and best-preserved of Europe's medieval castles—Château Vincennes—displays all of these classic features of castle architecture. Located not far east of Paris, France, the structure dates from 1150, with major additions completed in the early 1400s. The château's towering stone defensive walls, equipped with impressive machicolation, stretch for more than 0.5 miles (1km) and have six guard towers and three huge gates. Dwarfing all, however, is a massive stone tower situated inside the courtyard; the tallest fortified structure ever built in medieval Europe, it rises to a height of 171 feet (52m).

Early Christian Churches

Even as the first castles were sprouting up across Europe in early medieval times, monumental religious architecture was already evident in some places. In Rome's final century or so Christians gained control of the Roman government. And in the years following the Empire's disintegration Christianity became the dominant faith of Europe. In most parts of medieval Europe, therefore, religious architecture consisted of Christian churches and cathedrals.

Even before Rome's fall Christians were erecting large churches. Initially, for the sake of convenience they took over and refurbished existing Roman basilicas. This made sense from a logistical standpoint, since basilicas were big meeting places that could accommodate large numbers of people. As time went on, and new churches were built from scratch, the basic basilica form continued to be used. Certain changes were made, however. In front of the apse (semicircular recess at the back of nave) builders placed the altar. They also added a transept, a rectangular space crossing the nave at a right angle in front of the altar. Thereby, the nave and transept together formed a rudimentary cross, symbol of the faith.

Château Vincennes, depicted here in a nineteenth-century painting, has all of the classic features of castle architecture.

From an architectural standpoint, the culmination of early Christian architecture was Hagia Sophia, an enormous church in Constantinople, situated on the Bosphorus Strait in what was then northeastern Greece. After the fall of the western portion of the Roman Empire, the eastern portion rapidly mutated into the Greek-speaking Byzantine Empire. Byzantine Christian churches also utilized the basilica form. But they displayed many new additions and refinements. Chief among these was a huge dome soaring directly above the nave. Hagia Sophia's dome is 102 feet (31m) across and rests on four columns, each 70 feet (21m) tall. This architectural configuration—a dome placed atop a group of columns lining a square-shaped hall—became the most familiar trademark of Byzantine architecture. It produced a central interior space of great majesty, beauty, and spiritual inspiration. On seeing the completed Hagia Sophia, the early Byzantine historian Procopius remarked:

> The church has been made a spectacle of great beauty, stupendous to those who see it. . . . In the middle of the church there rise four [giant columns]. Upon these are

One awestruck writer described the enormous dome of the majestic Hagia Sophia as having the appearance of being "suspended from heaven."

placed four arches so as to form a square. . . . Above the arches, the construction rises in a circle [above which] is an enormous spherical dome which makes the building exceptionally beautiful. It seems not to be founded on solid masonry, but to be suspended from heaven.[25]

Romanesque and Gothic Architecture

Byzantine-style churches were erected throughout Greece and in neighboring parts of eastern Europe, as well as in Italy and

Sicily, in early medieval times. (Byzantine religious concepts and artistic styles also penetrated Russia, to the north, where the Russian Orthodox Church took root.) However, during these centuries western and northern Europe remained largely a separate cultural sphere. In general, the West had not yet fully recovered from the barbarian invasions that had toppled the western Roman Empire. And no towns or local nobles could afford to erect structures as large and splendid as Hagia Sophia. So, western Christian churches continued to employ mainly the converted basilica form on a relatively modest scale, usually with no dome. Most of these structures were, unlike Byzantine churches, rather plainly decorated.

This situation changed in a big way beginning in about the year 1000. In the century or so that followed, a massive burst of church building occurred in France and other parts of western Europe. "Each Christian people," a contemporary Christian monk wrote, "strove against the others to erect nobler [churches]. It was as if the whole Earth, having cast off the old by shaking itself, were clothing itself everywhere in the white robe of the church."[26]

The vigorous bout of church construction initiated what later historians dubbed the Romanesque period of art and architecture. It was characterized partly by the resemblance of the new churches to older Roman buildings. In particular, huge, rectangular blocks of stone and rounded arches, both trademarks of Roman construction, were in wide use. But the main differences between Romanesque structures and those that preceded them were size and ornamentation. The new churches were both larger and more highly decorated than earlier churches. "Interior surfaces were covered with wall paintings," architectural historian Michael Raeburn points out. "Porches, columns, [and] whole facades were decorated with sculpture and then painted, too."[27]

Saint-Sernin Basilica, completed in Toulouse, France, in 1120, remains one of the finest examples of Romanesque architecture. With a nave 377 feet (115m) long, it is much larger than any pre-Romanesque medieval French building. Also, both its interior and exterior are richly decorated. The altar is made of fine marble.

Fine marble, elaborate sculptures, and exquisite paintings decorate the Saint-Sernin Basilica, one of the finest examples of Romanesque architecture.

And the builders added nine small, elegant chapels, five accessible from the apse and two located in each wing of the transept. Outside, the front entrance is decorated with elaborate sculptures.

Not long after the cathedral at Saint-Sernin was completed, Europe's Romanesque style began to give way to an even more imposing style that later came to be called Gothic. Gothic churches first appeared in France in the twelfth century and continued to be built in Europe for several more centuries, even after the introduction of newer styles. Among the key differences between Romanesque and Gothic architecture are that Gothic added height, lightness of form, and large glass windows to let in more light. As noted architectural historians H.W. Janson and Anthony F. Janson put it: "The [Gothic] architectural forms seem graceful, almost weightless, against the massive solidity of the Romanesque, and the

TWO MEDIEVAL MASTER MASONS

Very few of the architects of Europe's medieval period (then called master masons) are known by name. Two of the few exceptions are Villard de Honnecourt (thirteenth century) and William of Sens (twelfth century), both Frenchmen. Nothing definite is known about Honnecourt's life, and he is known to later generations mainly because one of his sketchbooks has survived. It contains drawings of lifting devices, a mill-driven saw, and various buildings under construction. Some of these sketches reveal clues about some of the building methods of his time. One drawing—of a man wearing a tunic and a hat—may be a self-portrait. The life of William of Sens is also largely a mystery. But it is known that he rebuilt the choir of Canterbury Cathedral after it was destroyed in a fire. Also documented is that he suffered a serious injury after falling from the scaffolding erected for the job and was thereafter unable to work.

windows have been enlarged to the point that they . . . fill the entire wall area, so that they themselves become translucent walls."[28]

Another trademark of Gothic architecture is the flying buttress. Because Gothic cathedrals, such as Notre Dame in Paris, are so tall and broad, the immense weight of their upper sections pushes outward toward the sides. To counter this effect and thereby keep the building from falling down, medieval builders developed the flying buttress. This stone structure, engineering expert L. Sprague de Camp explains, is "like a

Flying buttresses help support the tall, broad walls of Notre Dame cathedral in France (illuminated in the foreground) and huge glass windows brighten the interior of Magdeburg's Cathedral in Germany (inset).

small section of an arch, leaning against the piers from outside the building, propping up the wall and counterbalancing the thrust of the roof vault."[29] Notre Dame was one of the first European cathedrals to utilize flying buttresses. They help hold up the walls and roof of the nave, which is an impressive 112 feet (34m) high.

Islamic Architecture

In the early centuries of Europe's medieval period, well before Notre Dame was erected, Muslim armies swept out of Arabia and conquered much of the Near East, North Africa, and southern Spain.

Hundreds of colored columns and arches grace the inside of the Great Mosque in Cordoba, Spain.

The Muslims not only introduced their religion, Islam, to these regions but also developed religious architecture used mainly in Islamic churches, called mosques. The Islamic architectural style was in many ways distinct from European styles. Muslim builders adopted architectural elements and ideas from various peoples, especially the Persians, Romans, Egyptians, and Byzantines. The Egyptian hypostyle hall, the Roman arch, and the Byzantine dome, for example, were incorporated into numerous Islamic structures. The result was a unique and elegant composite architectural approach.

Erected in the late 700s, one of the finest of all the medieval Islamic buildings is the Great Mosque at Cordoba in southern Spain. Inside its square-shaped interior is a hypostyle hall with hundreds of columns. Graceful arch-shaped ribs connect one column to another at the tops; and several other arches in the outer walls form doorways leading out into three courtyards. Eventually, a minaret was added to the structure. A trademark of Islamic architecture, a minaret is a tall tower from which a holy man known as a muezzin calls the faithful to prayer. In the centuries that followed, Muslim builders continued to employ arches, domes, and minarets, while farther north in Europe the Romanesque and Gothic styles were steadily overshadowed by the splendor of Renaissance architecture.

5

The Age of Domes: Europe's Renaissance

The final phase of Europe's medieval era is usually referred to as the Renaissance. From the standpoint of monumental architecture, the Renaissance lasted from about 1400 to 1600 and produced some of the most magnificent and memorable buildings in world history. The term *renaissance* means "rebirth." And the period was characterized by European artists and intellectuals rediscovering, or perhaps more accurately, reviving, the great artistic achievements of the ancient classical world, especially Rome. The widely influential Italian architect Andrea Palladio (1508–1580) declared:

> It was always my opinion that the ancient Romans, as in many other things, so in building as well, vastly excelled all those who have [existed] since their time. I proposed to myself [the Roman architect] Vitruvius as my master and guide . . . and set myself to search into the [details] of all the [surviving] ancient edifices. [30]

Space, Reason, Proportion, and Perspective

Palladio and his colleagues saw many things they admired in those ancient edifices, including arches, vaults, columns, domes, and other specific architectural elements. But what most impressed them were certain larger, less tangible concepts. Important among these was the use of space in the biggest ancient buildings. "The rediscovery of architectural space is the greatest achievement of Renaissance architecture," Michael Raeburn writes. "And although it needed a reversion to classical forms and classical simplicity to achieve it, these were only a means to an end, [as] the buildings of the early Renaissance were developments, not imitations, of Roman architecture."[31]

Yet it was not merely creating huge architectural spaces that set Renaissance buildings apart. After all, many earlier medieval structures, particularly Gothic cathedrals, featured truly enormous

The influential sixteenth-century architect Andrea Palladio redesigned the Church of San Giorgio Maggiore (pictured) in Venice, Italy.

interior spaces. What made Renaissance architecture different was a striving to make these spaces balanced, proportioned, and symmetrical both logically and mathematically. Gothic interior spaces had no set rules of proportion; they were shaped more by the heart and religious faith than by reason. In contrast, Renaissance architects held that good architecture should be built on mathematical ratios expressed in whole numbers—such as 1 to 2, 2 to 4, and so forth. This approach would allow human-made structures to display a sort of natural beauty, since it was widely believed that such ratios were inherent in nature itself. "There is a certain excellence and natural beauty in the figures and forms of buildings," Alberti wrote. This innate beauty "strikes the mind with pleasure and admiration." It is a sense of right proportions and harmony that comes "from nature, so that its true seat is in the mind and in reason. This is what architecture chiefly aims at, and by this she obtains her beauty, dignity, and value."[32]

This preoccupation with harmony, proportion, and mathematics was partly expressed through the exploitation of the visual effect of perspective. Indeed, "the Renaissance was in love with perspective," as Anita Abramovitz puts it.

> Before the Renaissance era, artists and builders had been aware intuitively that objects at a distance were seen as smaller than those in the foreground. And this awareness was shown in their drawings. However, the Renaissance is credited with the "discovery" of perspective because perspective was developed then as a geometric principle and an optical theory, and it established mathematically the relative dimensions of objects in three-dimensional space.[33]

Thus, Renaissance architects employed perspective to achieve an overall visual effect. The sizes and placement of doors, windows, stairways, terraces, balustrades, columns, and other architectural elements were chosen to create an integrated overall effect that was both pleasing and dramatic.

Although doors, windows, and stairways are elements common to nearly all styles of architecture, Renaissance architects strongly emphasized certain other elements. Among these

To achieve a pleasing but dramatic effect, Renaissance architects emphasized harmony and proportion, as can be seen in Italy's Palazzo Vecchio (pictured).

was frequent use of Greco-Roman pediments, or variations of them, in building facades. Columns, utilizing the ancient Doric, Ionic, and Corinthian orders, or composites of them, were also common elements of both the exteriors and interiors of Renaissance buildings. Most often such columns were load-bearing, that is, they supported upper stories or roofs. However, Renaissance architecture also made widespread use of pilasters—non-load-bearing, flattened or abbreviated columns attached to outer or inner walls mainly for decoration. Renaissance interiors also featured decorative effects such as frescoes (paintings done on wet plaster) and richly detailed moldings. In addition, domes, based on Roman models, became popular for the exteriors of Renaissance buildings. Moreover, Renaissance builders used domes, pediments, columns, pilasters, and railed balustrades not only for churches but also for secular structures such as palaces, private villas, libraries, hospitals, and all manner of public buildings.

Brunelleschi's Dome

It was, nevertheless, a church and the special requirements of its dome that inspired the first significant architectural achievement of the Renaissance. The events in question took place in the city-state of Florence, in north-central Italy, which became the initial focus of architectural activity in that period. By the late 1300s Florence had become a major European center of learning as well as a military power that competed for political dominance with other Italian states. And to increase their prestige the Florentines poured large sums of money into large-scale construction projects.

One such project was the city's huge new cathedral, the Basilica of Saint Mary of the Flowers. Work on the structure had begun in the late 1200s and continued off and on for more than a century. By 1418 all that was left to erect was the dome, which according to the design had to be 137 feet (42m) wide at the base. The problem was that no one in Europe had built such an enormous dome during the previous nine hundred years, and local architects were uncertain as to how to go about it. The government therefore held a contest for the best design. The

winner was Filippo Brunelleschi (1337–1446), who turned out to be the first great architect of the Renaissance.

In tackling this formidable challenge, Brunelleschi drew inspiration mainly from the great dome of the ancient Pantheon in Rome. That large, spherical structure was still in use in the fifteenth century (and remains in excellent condition today). Brunelleschi observed that one reason that the Pantheon's dome had remained intact for so many centuries was that the builders had coffered the stones making up its bulk. That is, they had partly hollowed out each stone, thereby greatly reducing the dome's overall weight.

To achieve even more weight reduction in his own dome, Brunelleschi devised a design featuring two relatively thin masonry (stone and brick) domes, one encasing the other. A series of iron and stone ribs connect the inner dome to the outer one, leaving mostly empty space between. In this ingenious

Architect Filippo Brunelleschi solved the problem of how to design the dome of the Basilica of Saint Mary of the Flowers (pictured).

THE GOLDSMITH WHO BECAME AN ARCHITECT

Filippo Brunelleschi (1377–1446) was the first prominent architect of Europe's Renaissance. Born in Florence, as a young man he became a goldsmith. Between 1402 and 1404, however, he traveled to Rome, along with his friend, the famous painter Donatello, to study the many ancient Roman ruins there. Greatly inspired, Brunelleschi, then about twenty-six or so, decided to become an architect. He received his first commission to erect a building in 1419. That structure, Florence's Foundling Hospital, was the first in the city to feature Greco-Roman–style columns, which thereafter became hallmarks of Renaissance architecture. That same year Brunelleschi won a government-sponsored contest for the best design for the dome of the local cathedral. That monumental project was completed in 1436. Two churches he designed in Florence—Saint Lorenzo and Saint Mary of the Holy Spirit—profoundly inspired later Renaissance architects and builders. A multi-talented individual, Brunelleschi also designed mechanical hoists, fortifications for his home town, and theatrical props and machines used in religious plays.

arrangement, the domes reinforce each other, while the ribs carry most of their weight downward onto eight massive piers embedded in the walls below the dome. This redistribution of weight was imperative. Even factoring in the weight reduction afforded by the design, the combined domes are still phenomenally heavy at 40,785 tons (37,000t).

Revolutionary Symmetry

Brunelleschi completed the new dome in 1436. During the construction process he had invented several special hoisting machines to lift the materials high above the cathedral floor. These became models for hoists used by builders across Europe during the Renaissance. Brunelleschi himself employed them on his own later buildings. Among the more splendid and influential of these was another church—San Lorenzo (the Basilica of Saint Lawrence), also in Florence. Work began in the 1420s while Saint Mary's great dome was still under construction.

The floor plan for San Lorenzo demonstrates the emphasis that Brunelleschi and other Renaissance architects placed on mathematical ratios and proportions. At first glance the plan looks similar to the layout of many Romanesque and Gothic churches, with a long nave crossed by a rectangular transept. However, a closer look reveals a radically new approach in which the interior space is divided into a number of square-shaped units. These are of varying sizes and arranged in a perfectly symmetrical pattern. "Four large squares form the choir [in the apse, in the rear] and the arms of the transept," the Jansons point out.

Filippo Brunelleschi emphasized ratios and proportions in the design of the church known as San Lorenzo (pictured) in Florence, Italy.

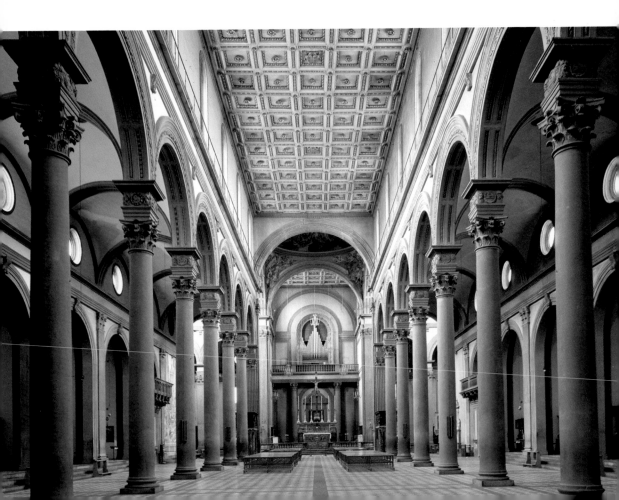

Four more are combined into the nave. Other squares, one-fourth the size of the large ones, make up the aisles and the chapels attached to the transept. . . . In other words, Brunelleschi conceived Saint Lorenzo as a grouping of abstract "space blocks," the larger ones being simple multiples of the standard unit. Once we understand this, we realize how revolutionary he was. [34]

This logical mathematical approach, along with the general plan of Saint Lorenzo and some other Florentine churches Brunelleschi designed, were widely copied throughout Europe in the centuries that followed.

Classical-Style Exteriors

Brunelleschi's overall legacy was the introduction of many innovative and influential ideas about the structural elements and interior spaces of buildings. How he viewed and fashioned the exteriors of his buildings is little known, however. This is because most of these exteriors were never finished or have not survived. It was the next giant of Renaissance architecture, Leon Battista Alberti, who found workable, elegant ways to apply classical architectural elements to the exteriors of nonclassical structures.

One of Alberti's answers to this challenge can be seen in his Palazzo Rucellai in Florence, completed in 1451. (Although the Italian term *palazzo* translates literally as "palace," not all palazzos were palaces; in Italy and surrounding lands, the term was used more generally to denote a large, grand building.) The elements in the building's facade were inspired by those the Romans had used in the famous Colosseum. The exterior of the great amphitheater consisted of several levels, each bearing rows of arches separated by columns and pilasters. The front of Alberti's palazzo mimics this arrangement. It has three stories, each oversized, and the windows on the upper two stories are encased in arches, each framed by elegant pilasters.

A similar challenge materialized when the chief nobleman of the town of Rimini, in northeastern Italy, asked Alberti to renovate the basilica-style Church of Francesco. The new building was to be a tomb and monument to the memory of the nobleman and his family. In brilliant fashion, Alberti encased the older structure in a shell shaped like a modified ancient Roman temple. The front door has a pediment above it and rests within a huge arch reminiscent of the triumphal arches through which victorious Roman armies marched. Many other such arches, along with several towering Corinthian columns, run around the building's perimeter. In this way, Alberti achieved his goal of superimposing a classical temple on a medieval basilica.

Michelangelo and the Mannerists

In certain ways, the great Italian artist, sculptor, and architect Michelangelo Buonarotti (1475–1564) perpetuated the architectural styles and ideas developed by Brunelleschi, Alberti, and other earlier Renaissance masters. For example, one of the great facades

THE RENAISSANCE'S SUPREME ARTIST

The name and reputation of Michelangelo Buonarotti (1475–1564) looms large in the annals of Western art. Born in a small town in Tuscany, in north-central Italy, he grew up in Florence. As a young man he became an architect, painter, and sculptor of extraordinary skill and in his lifetime produced some of the finest works of Europe's Renaissance. As an architect, he designed the dome for Saint Peter's Basilica in Rome; the magnificent town square known as the Campidoglio, also in Rome; and the Laurentian Library and Medici Chapel, both part of the San Lorenzo church complex in Florence. As a sculptor, Michelangelo created a huge statue of the biblical character David that stands 14 feet (4.2m) high and the breathtaking *Pietà*, showing Mary holding the dead body of her son Jesus. And as a painter, Michelangelo is most famous for his large series of painted panels on the ceiling of the Sistine Chapel in the Vatican in Rome. The most renowned of these panels depicts God endowing the first human, Adam, with the spark of life.

Michelangelo erected in the splendid town square he designed, the Campidoglio, resembles the front of Alberti's Palazzo Rucellai. (Work on the Campidoglio, at the summit of Rome's Capitoline Hill, began in the 1540s.) The facade is much larger and more visually dramatic than Alberti's palazzo, however. Its windows, like those in the palazzo, are encased in arches with pilasters set between each. But Michelangelo's pilasters are far larger. Each topped by a Corinthian capital, they stretch all the way from the ground to the underside of the roof, conveying an overpowering feeling of grandeur and solidity.

Michelangelo's theatricality and innovative ideas are even more evident in the interior spaces he created for the Laurentian Library in Florence (built between 1524 and 1533). The entrance hall leading to the main section of the library consists of a conglomeration of classical architectural elements combined and positioned in very unclassical ways. The columns on either side of the door, for instance, are recessed into the wall instead of pro-

In architecture, Michelangelo preferred self-expression over function and symmetry as can be seen in his design of the central staircase in the Laurentian Library.

THE AMAZING DOME AT SAINT PETER'S

One of the most impressive architectural achievements of the Renaissance was the dome, or cupola, of Saint Peter's Basilica in Rome. The dome was designed by Michelangelo. But at the time of his death in 1564, only its supports had been constructed. Additions to the design were made between 1585 and 1590 by architect Giacomo della Porta and engineer Domenico Fontana. The finished product was a double dome like that erected earlier in Florence by Brunelleschi. The diameter of St. Peter's dome's interior space is 139 feet (42.5m) and its highest interior point soars an amazing 394 feet (120m) above the floor. This famous structure became the inspiration for many large domes built later across the globe, notably those of Saint Paul's Cathedral in London and the U.S. Capitol in Washington, D.C.

Michelangelo designed the magnificent dome of St. Peter's Basilica (shown).

jected outward from it. Also, the pilasters on the walls are unevenly spaced and taper downward, something never seen in Greco-Roman versions. In addition, the central staircase leading to the door widens as it moves downward, and the stairs are of increasingly unequal widths and curved rather than rectangular. "Walking up or down this amazing structure," Frederick Hartt observes, "is an experience so disturbing as to leave little doubt that the harmonies" of earlier Renaissance buildings "have been left far behind."[35]

Clearly, in shaping the interiors of the Laurentian Library and some of his other architectural works, Michelangelo was interested less in function and symmetry and more in expressing his individuality and creative side. For this reason, he is often categorized as a mannerist. Mannerism was a sub-period of Renaissance art lasting from about 1520 to 1600. Mannerists continued to use classical elements, as Michelangelo did in the library hall, but they tended to experiment more than their immediate predecessors. In so doing, their works were often more eclectic (mixing diverse ideas or styles), novel, and theatrical and featured exaggerated or less harmonious proportions.

One of the more successful of the mannerists, Giorgio Vasari (1511–1574), was strongly influenced by Michelangelo. Vasari utilized the idea of recessed columns, for instance, in the facades of the Palazzo degli Uffizi. The structure consists of two long, three-story municipal office buildings facing each other across a narrow public walkway. Although these facades superficially resemble that of Alberti's Palazzo Rucellai, their decorations are much busier with detail, including several statues standing in recessed niches.

This trend of exaggeration and novelty in monumental architecture was destined to continue and intensify. As a result, as Europe emerged into the early modern era in the 1600s, it remained the world's center of architectural experimentation and innovation. The pursuit of newness, expressed in a parade of ever-changing styles, had become part of the DNA, so to speak, of Western architecture.

Idealizing the Past: The Early Modern Period

In the fine arts, including painting, sculpture, and architecture, the years from the end of the Renaissance in 1600 to about 1900 are often termed the early modern period. During these three centuries European architectural styles continued to evolve. At the same time, these styles were adopted in many of the lands that European nations colonized in this age, including British colonial America (later the United States), Canada, Australia, and others. Along with political, religious, and literary ideas, architecture was a major element in the spread of Western culture across large sections of the globe.

Not surprisingly, the globalization of Western ideas imparted a certain degree of cultural sameness in all Western societies. There was also a degree of sameness in most of the architectural styles that developed in the early modern period. True, each of these styles—among them baroque, rococo, and neoclassical—had specific elements and characteristics that set it apart from the others. Yet, all were to one degree or another outgrowths of, or variations on, the styles of the Renaissance. Therefore, Greco-Roman influence, the main inspiration for the Renaissance, remained strong in Western architecture. Nostalgia for past architectural styles also instigated various revivals in the early modern period. Perhaps the most famous was the Gothic revival that reached its peak in the late nineteenth century.

Saint Paul's Cathedral in London combines elements of Neoclassical, Gothic, and Baroque architectural styles.

Baroque: A Fusion of Art Forms

The first major architectural style of the early modern period was not a revival but an elaboration of mannerism, the final phase of the Renaissance. The new style, dubbed "baroque," thrived from roughly 1600 to the mid-1700s. To the untrained eye, mannerist and baroque structures can appear very similar. And the differences are largely matters of degree and intent. Just as the mannerists exaggerated many elements of Renaissance architecture, so too did baroque architects exaggerate the mannerist style. On the whole, baroque architecture is characterized by themes and feelings of lofty drama and theatricality, an extreme degree of detail and ornamentation, and a marked indulgence in personal expression by the architects. Indeed, "Baroque at its height represented self-expression gone wild," one expert observer remarks. Its use of "dramatic effects of light and shadow" and "often overwhelming decoration" were often intended to produce "a sensational emotional effect."[36]

Also, in their utilization of a profusion of detailed decoration, baroque buildings often made sculptures and paintings nearly as prominent as standard architectural elements. Thus, the baroque period of art witnessed a sort of fusion of the artistic disciplines of architecture, sculpture, and painting. This often sumptuous-looking mixture of art forms is well illustrated in the tabernacle (altar and choir area) in Saint Peter's Basilica in Rome. Completed in 1633, it was designed by the great Italian sculptor and architect Giovanni

With its dramatic ornamentation and elaborate design, the tabernacle of St. Peter's Basilica is a good example of the baroque style.

Architect Giovanni Lorenzo Bernini designed the Cornaro Chapel at Santa Maria della Vittoria as a showpiece for his sculpture, *The Ecstasy of Saint Theresa.*

Lorenzo Bernini (1598–1680). The Jansons describe this landmark artwork:

> The tabernacle is a splendid fusion of architecture and sculpture. Four ornate, spiral-shaped columns support an upper platform. At its corners are statues of angels and vigorously carved scrolls which raise high the symbol of the victory of Christianity over the pagan world, a cross above a golden orb. The entire structure is so alive with expressive energy that it strikes us as the very epitome [perfect example] of Baroque style.[37]

Incredibly, Bernini managed to surpass his work at Saint Peter's in his architectural masterpiece—the Cornaro Chapel at Santa Maria della Vittoria in Rome, completed in 1652. Here, he designed the entire structure to house and show off the qualities of his magnificent sculpture, *The Ecstasy of Saint Theresa*. The ceiling is a great barrel vault covered with painted clouds, rays of sunlight, and flying angels. Far beneath, to the rear of the altar, the *Ecstasy* rests in a recessed niche surrounded by ornate Corinthian columns and layer upon layer of splendidly decorated moldings and other architectural, sculptural, and painted details.

Rococo: Lightness and Intimate Detail

The last thirty to forty years of the baroque period of European art are usually viewed separately as a sub-period known as rococo. That term derived from a combination of the Italian word barocco, meaning "baroque," and the French word rocaille, meaning "shell." (Sea shells are curved, and rococo art is partly characterized by moldings and other decorations that curve and flow.) Rococo architecture carried on the merger of artistic fields and explosion of detail seen in baroque structures.

However, rococo did this on a considerably smaller, lighter, more intimate, and more delicate scale. Used most frequently in the design of the interiors of palaces, hotels, and expensive homes, rococo frequently extended the baroque fusion of art forms to include such details as fine furniture, tapestries, carpets, and dinnerware. Goldsmiths, silversmiths, wood carvers, upholsterers, painters, sculptors, glassmakers, and many other artisans contributed their talents to support the architect's overall vision. This vision was nothing less than a total interior environment aiming to provide the ultimate in comfort and elegance. Needless to say, the homes and hotels designed and built in this style catered only to the well-to-do.

A typical example of a classic rococo interior space is the Hôtel de Varengeville in Paris (ca. 1735), designed by French architect Nicolas Pineau (1684–1754). Most of the original guest rooms were long ago ransacked or redecorated. But one of these rooms was painstakingly reconstructed in the modern era. It has a high ceiling with elaborate bronze-encrusted moldings running along its edges and several huge mirrors, also rimmed with bronze decorations. A lovely marble fireplace faces a magnificent hand-carved wooden table, which sits on an equally richly detailed handmade carpet. Above the table hangs a chandelier composed of a mass of finely wrought crystal and bronze. In addition, ornate statues and paintings are strategically placed throughout the room to enhance the overall effect of extreme elegance.

Neoclassicism: A Return to Sobriety

In the rococo style, European architects refined and decorated Renaissance and baroque structures with so much attention to detail that there was simply no way to make them any more elaborate. With seemingly nowhere left to go in this direction, a reaction set in. In some ways it can be seen as a reversal of direction, or a return to the more basic and substantial classical architectural forms created during the Renaissance. Appropriately, therefore, the new period, or style, of architecture came to be called neoclassicism. It lasted roughly from the mid-1700s to the late nineteenth century.

On the one hand, neoclassical architects aimed to revive Greco-Roman themes and elements that were more serious and less mired down in what came to be seen as the frivolous detail of the baroque and rococo periods. Neoclassic was "a more sober architecture," James Neal writes, "reflective of the ponderous [European] political empires that were now exerting their power" over large parts of the globe. "There was a need in the turbulent times for an architecture that showed permanence and stability, a far cry from the gaiety of Baroque and Rococo."[38]

One of the cultural motivations for the outburst of neoclassical architecture was the discovery of Pompeii and Herculaneum in the mid-1700s. These ancient Roman towns had been buried during a large volcanic eruption in the first century A.D. Seeing the emerging ruins of the buried towns, European architects were inspired to recapture the "glory of Greece" and "grandeur of Rome."

But an even more potent inspiration for neoclassical architects consisted of the works of the late Renaissance architect Andrea Palladio. The facades of his buildings had quite often

Renaissance architect Andrea Palladio's work, especially his building facades and windows (pictured), influenced neoclassical styles.

featured a row of columns topped by a triangular pediment—an architectural form borrowed directly from the front porches of Greco-Roman temples. Another of Palladio's trademarks had been his windows. A Palladian window (sometimes called a Venetian window) was topped by a Roman arch, flanked by decorative pilasters, and usually had a balustrade projecting from the bottom.

English and American Neoclassicism

Neoclassical buildings borrowing these and other classical architectural elements were erected across large portions of Europe as well as the Untied States and other lands originally settled by Europeans. Such structures were particularly popular in England, where the style was first applied in a big way. The first outstanding example was Chiswick House near London, begun in 1725 and designed by Richard Boyle, better known as Lord Burlington (1694–1753). The house's front porch consists of a Palladian-style temple facade fronted by a row of six columns and topped by a sparsely decorated pediment. Stairways with elegant balustrades flow downward from each side of the porch; they are evenly spaced, as neoclassicism strove to revive the classical concept of symmetry that mannerist and baroque builders had often ignored. Behind the front porch, above the main section of the house, looms a modest, unornamented dome. Overall, the structure exudes a sense of balance and restraint almost never seen in baroque structures.

Though the distinctive look of Chiswick House's exterior was frequently reproduced (with some variations) in later neoclassical buildings, the architects of the era did not ignore the interiors of these structures. One of the finest examples of neoclassical interior design is the library for Kenwood House in London, completed in 1769. The architect was Robert Adam (1728–1792), widely seen as the dominant figure in European neoclassical architecture. The symmetrical rectangular main room features a barrel-vaulted ceiling. And a row of Corinthian columns on one side opens into a semicircular apse lined with bookshelves. Impeccably decorated in a color scheme of white, muted blue, and red, with gold highlights, Adam's library is essentially an ancient Roman interior modified to meet the needs of an upper-class eighteenth-century gentleman.

It was probably inevitable that Lord Burlington, Robert Adam, and other leading English neoclassicists would exert an influence on builders in England's colonies. And when the thirteen American colonies broke away and became the United States in 1776, that influence remained strong. There, the neoclassical/Palladian style became known as Georgian. Among the leading early U.S. architects was Thomas Jefferson, author of the Declaration of Independence and the new country's third president. His Virginia home, Monticello, begun in the late 1700s, was inspired by Chiswick House and other Palladian structures. Jefferson's front porch features four Doric columns topped by a simple pediment;

ROBERT ADAM

Born in Scotland, Robert Adam (1728–1792) is often called the greatest architect of the late eighteenth century and the leading proponent of the neoclassical architectural style. His interest in designing buildings came from his father, an architect and stonemason. (Robert Adam's younger bother, James, also became an architect and the two eventually became partners in a family architectural firm.) After getting an education in Britain, Robert Adam spent long periods in France and Italy studying ancient Roman ruins, which inspired him to use classical elements in contemporary buildings. Many of these elements, including Greco-Roman columns, pediments, and domes, came to grace the upper-class British homes Adam built or remodeled. After his death he was given the high honor of burial in London's Westmintser Abbey. And his surviving drawings are now on display in the Soane Museum, also in London.

Chiswick House in Chiswick, England, designed by Lord Burlington, influenced U.S. president Thomas Jefferson's design of his home, Monticello.

a modest but lovely dome resting on an octagonal red brick base rises from the center of the house.

Jefferson utilized a similar design, though on a larger scale, for the rotunda of the University of Virginia, completed in 1825. His love for the Greco-Roman style is evident in a statement he made about how the yet-to-be-built U.S. Capitol should look: "Whenever it is proposed to prepare plans for the Capitol, I should prefer the adoption of some one of the [classical] models of antiquity which have had the [approval and praise] of thousands of years."[39]

The Gothic Revival

Although neoclassicism was a major force in architecture in the eighteenth and nineteenth centuries, it was not the only style chosen for monumental buildings. Many Gothic-style structures were also erected in this period. Although largely superseded by the Renaissance style back in the fifteenth and sixteenth centuries, Gothic architecture did not completely die out in Europe. And a few Gothic buildings were built during the baroque period. (For example, the universities of Cambridge and Oxford, in England, added several Gothic-style structures in the 1600s.) Then in the eighteenth century came the emergence of Gothic literature, which romanticized the medieval era. This stimulated a reawakening of interest in Gothic architecture, a popular movement that came to be called the Gothic revival, or the neo-Gothic style. Some

JEFFERSON ADOPTS NEOCLASSICISM

Thomas Jefferson (1743–1826), one of the founding fathers of the United States, was a capable architect who fell in love with the architectural styles of the ancient Greeks and Romans. This brief summary of how he came to adopt those styles comes from UNESCO's World Heritage List.

Jefferson's use of Roman classical forms initially was inspired by a love of classical language, philosophy, and arts gained through books. He was so enamored of classical literature that, in his lifetime, he read more of it than the average professional classicist. Jefferson also desired to raise American architecture to a level comparable to European architecture. During five years in Paris, from 1784 to 1789, [he] studied both Roman buildings and the French use of Roman orders in new architecture. He returned to the United States with these lessons and transformed his house at Monticello into a unique adaptation of the Neo-Classical villa. The University of Virginia was Jefferson's last major architectural project. The original campus represents an unusual translation of Roman classical forms to a hilly site and to the requirements of a community of scholars.

UNESCO, "World Heritage List Nomination: Monticello and the University of Virginia in Charlottesville." whc.unesco.org/sites/nom/us-jef.htm.

scholars estimate that more Gothic buildings were constructed after 1750 in Europe and North America than were built in medieval times.

Among the finest of these structures is Manchester Town Hall in Manchester, England, designed by Alfred Waterhouse and completed in 1877. It is dominated by a bell tower 280 feet (85m) high with an enormous clock set in the front wall. An even taller tower, topped by a pointed Gothic spire, graces St. James's Cathedral in Toronto, Canada. Designed by Frederick Cumberland and completed in 1844, the spire soars to a height

Manchester Town Hall in England, designed in the neo-Gothic style, dominates Manchester's town square.

of 305 feet (93m). Perhaps most imposing of all is St. Patrick's Cathedral in New York City, completed by architect James Renwick in 1878. Its twin towers, reminiscent of those of Paris's Notre Dame Cathedral, are 330 feet (100m) high.

A Foreshadowing of Things to Come

Some of the later structures of the Gothic revival possessed a crucial quality that no earlier versions did. Namely, they had partial or full iron frames. The Industrial Revolution, which flourished in Europe and North America in the 1800s, introduced new, stronger, more flexible building materials, including iron, which began to be used extensively in railways, bridges, and ships.

In the realm of monumental architecture, particularly influential was the Crystal Palace. Designed by Joseph Paxton and erected in London's Hyde Park for the Great Exhibition of 1851, it was 1,850 feet (560m) long, 110 feet (33m) high, and covered 25 acres (10ha). The Crystal Palace was composed almost entirely of iron girders and large glass panels. This advanced and innovative mode of construction foreshadowed the widespread use of iron girders and glass in the modern era. At the time, no one could guess that the age of the skyscraper was just around the proverbial corner.

New Innovations: The Twentieth Century and Beyond

L ondon's Crystal Palace had demonstrated more than the potential of iron and glass in building construction. It had also shown the tremendous usefulness of prefabricated (or pre-fab) materials, that is, premade, mass-produced units. Such units could be made in a factory by the hundreds or thousands, shipped to a construction site, and assembled according to the architect's preset plan. Utilizing many prefab units, the Crystal Palace had taken only nine months to erect. Moreover, it could be easily dis-mantled and moved. (In fact, it was moved to a new location a few years after the Great Exhibition closed. The building *was* final-ly destroyed by fire in 1936.)

Prefab iron girders were also used to stunning effect in the now-famous Eiffel Tower in Paris. Designed by French archi-tect Alexandre-Gustave Eiffel and completed in 1889, it is 1,063 feet (324m) high. The tower's 8,000-ton mass (7,200t) rests on four immense concrete foundations buried in the ground beneath the structure. Eiffel's creation, which became an enduring French landmark and trademark, remained the tallest human-made structure in world for the next forty-one years.

Three new technological advances had made a very tall struc-ture such as the Eiffel Tower possible. One was the advent of the elevator, invented in the 1850s and made widely available by 1880. This invention allowed both construction workers and those who would later use a building to reach higher levels with ease. The other two advances were new materials, steel and reinforced concrete. Steel was produced by adding small amounts of carbon to iron, making it harder, more flexible, and increasing its tensile strength. Reinforced concrete was made by adding iron or steel rods to concrete, greatly increasing its strength and stability. On the advantages of reinforced concrete, engineer and architect Mario Salvadori writes:

> It can be poured into forms and given any shape suitable to the channeling of loads. It can be sculpted to the wishes of the architect. . . . It is economical, available almost everywhere, fire-resistant, and can be designed to be lightweight to reduce the dead load or to have a whole gamut [range] of strengths to satisfy structural needs. [40]

Known to people the world over, the Eiffel Tower rises 1,063 feet above Paris.

These key innovations—reinforced concrete, steel, and the elevator—opened the way for an exciting new age of architecture and construction that is still in full swing today.

The Chicago Style and Traditionalism

In the late 1880s some architects began to use these modern advances in big commercial and civic buildings to create large amounts of interior space. Importantly, the tensile strength of steel and reinforced concrete removed the need for the outer walls of these structures to bear a large portion of the overall load. Instead, most of the load could be distributed evenly through an interior framework made of steel and strengthened by reinforced concrete. In turn, this allowed architects to concentrate on added vertical height without fear of the structure collapsing. So buildings got taller and taller.

Because the early leading proponents of this new approach were architects based in Chicago, it became known as the "Chicago style," which flourished from the late 1880s to about 1930. Its emergence in Chicago was no accident. In 1871 large portions of the city had been demolished in the famous Chicago Fire. And this had created an unprecedented opportunity for architects and builders to fill large spaces with new and hopefully innovative monumental structures.

The first outstanding example was Chicago's Home Insurance Building, designed in the 1880s by William LeBaron Jenney (1832–1907). It had ten stories and stood 138 feet (42m) high. Considerably taller was another Chicago building, the Masonic Temple (1892). Designed by Daniel Burnham (1846–1912), it had twenty-two stories and was 302 feet (92m) high. This made it the world's tallest building (excluding the Eiffel Tower, which was not seen as a traditional building) until it was surpassed in 1894 by the Manhattan Life Building in New York City.

These large commercial structures featured a fair amount of traditional architectural decoration on their exteriors. For example, the Masonic Temple's front door was encased in a Roman-style stone arch, with smaller decorative arches lining the street floor on either side. Meanwhile, the top few floors and roof were heavily decorated with modified Gothic and classical elements. The early years of the twentieth century witnessed not only increasingly tall steel-framed buildings but also a continuation of the use of these sorts of traditional outer decorations. And appropriately, some architectural historians came to call such structures "traditionalist." Concisely summing up this approach, Trachtenberg and Hyman say that it "accommodated new building types within old fashioned covers."[41]

A series of early skyscrapers in New York City typified the traditionalist style. The Woolworth Building, raised in 1913 and designed by Cass Gilbert (1859–1934), was the first true skyscraper. It stands 792 feet (241m) high and cost the then-huge sum of $13,500,000 to build. Gilbert purposely gave the structure a Gothic look by placing a Gothic-style tower on top of its lower half, which consists of a massive rectangular base. Though it is an office building, its resemblance to a Gothic cathedral has inspired some people to call it a "cathedral of commerce."

The Woolworth Building remained the tallest building in the world until 40 Wall Street and the Chrysler Building were erected in 1929–1930. The Chrysler Building, at a height of seventy-seven stories and 1,170 feet (357m, counting its topmost spire),

Geometric shapes, sweeping curves, and sunburst patterns can be found in the Art Deco styling of the Chrysler building (shown) in New York City. Inset shows exterior detail from the building.

was not only the tallest building in the world at the time but also the tallest structure, surpassing the Eiffel Tower. Designed by William Van Alen, the new skyscraper was a particularly successful traditionalist structure with some unique and quirky traits that put it in a sort of class by itself. These traits were part of a then popular artistic style called Art Deco. It was characterized by an eclectic combination of geometric shapes, especially zigzags, sweeping curves (including vaulted ceilings), and hemispheres and sunburst patterns, all influenced by machines and machine parts. Art Deco also featured liberal use of shiny aluminum and stainless steel and interior spaces decorated with gaudy colors.

The Chrysler Building did not hold onto its title of world's tallest structure for long. In May 1931 New York's Empire State Building was completed. Another traditionalist skyscraper in the Art Deco style, it was designed by the architectural firm of Shreve, Lamb, and Harmon. It has 102 stories, stands 1,250 feet (381m) tall (1,453 feet [443m], counting a broadcast tower later added at the top), and has sixty-five hundred windows and seventy-three elevators.

Frank Lloyd Wright and Private Houses

Less traditional in his approach to designing buildings was an American, Frank Lloyd Wright (1867–1959), widely viewed as one of the leading and most influential architects of the twentieth century. He was initially trained in the Chicago style and for a while worked with leading proponents of that approach, including Louis Sullivan (1856–1924). But soon Wright struck out on his own. Thereafter, with some notable exceptions, he concentrated more on private houses and smaller structures rather than office buildings and other monumental structures. Yet like the architects of larger buildings, Wright utilized modern materials, including steel frames, reinforced concrete, glass panels, and so forth. Wright's smaller structures also incorporated stone, wood, and other natural materials in an effort to appeal to the needs and comforts of the families who lived in them.

FRANK LLOYD WRIGHT

*O*ne of the most prominent architects of the first half of the twentieth century, Frank Lloyd Wright (1867–1959) was born in a small town in Wisconsin. When he was a child his mother gave him a set of toy building blocks having geometrical shapes. He later recalled that his experimentation with these blocks helped him form some of his early architectural ideas. After attending an engineering school in Wisconsin, in 1887 Wright moved to Chicago and joined a respected architectural firm. Six years later he left the firm and set up his own practice in Oak Park, a Chicago suburb. By 1901 he had designed about fifty homes, mostly in the immediate region. And between that time and 1917 he designed many more houses in what came to be called the Prairie style. The best known of the many private residences Wright designed were erected between 1935 and 1939, including Fallingwater in Pennsylvania. But his masterpiece remains the Solomon R. Guggenheim Museum in New York City, completed in 1959 shortly before his death. Designed to resemble a giant seashell, its interior features a large-scale rising spiral ramp.

This led Wright to create the so-called Prairie style of domestic architecture. It consists of a longish rectangular shell, often with one or more rectangular wings, topped by a low, sloping roof composed of stone or concrete slabs. Wright's houses typically featured extensive use of terraces covered by overhanging roof sections. An important example of his Prairie architecture is Robie House in Chicago, built in 1910. Made of fired bricks, sandstone slabs, wood, and glass, it is now a national historic landmark.

The most famous of Wright's private dwellings is Fallingwater, built for Mr. and Mrs. E.J. Kaufmann in Bear Run, Pennsylvania. The goal was to place the occupants as close to

The Frank Lloyd Wright house known as Fallingwater (shown) appears to have grown out of the natural surroundings.

nature as possible. This was accomplished by setting the house in a thick stand of trees and allowing a stream with a waterfall to run directly beneath part of the house. Wright's attempt to make buildings seem to grow naturally out their surroundings became known informally as "organic" architecture. Modified versions of Wright's houses were erected, copied, and recopied by house builders across the United States and beyond all through the twentieth century.

The International Style

Meanwhile, in the realm of larger-scale, commercial architecture, the Chicago and traditionalist styles were giving way to a new form known as modernism (or modern architecture). Modernist architects disliked the older styles, viewing them as derivative (copied and unoriginal), too beholden to frivolous decoration, and in general outmoded. The newer style had a more formal, often spare and non-aesthetic look. It was characterized by extreme simplicity of form and a rejection of ornamentation and decoration. Modernist buildings used a lot of steel, glass, concrete, and prefabricated, mass-produced materials and most often looked like huge unadorned boxes, slabs, or monoliths. Modernist architects also promoted an idealistic notion that this new style would serve the needs of and please the vast majority of the general public. In that regard, they expressed an ill-defined, equally idealistic belief that modernism represented the wave of architecture's future for centuries to come.

Among the more important early proponents of modernism were France's Charles E. Jeanneret, better known as "Le Corbusier" (1887–1965), and Germany's Walter Gropius (1883–1969) and Ludwig Mies van der Rohe (1886–1969). The latter two were strongly influenced by Frank Lloyd Wright. The new movement began in the years following World War I and reached its stride between 1930 and 1960. During these years it became the most dominant style in the world for large-scale civic and commercial structures, especially in Europe, North and South America, and the Soviet Union. For this reason, it came to be called the International Style.

Many thousands of large buildings were erected in this architectural form. Among the more familiar commercial versions are the United Nations (UN) Headquarters (1952), the Seagram Building (1958), Lever House (1952), and the Pan Am Building (1963), all in New York City; and IBM Plaza (1973) in Chicago. The style was also widely used for giant urban housing projects in cities across the globe.

The New Architectural Revolution

Despite the idealism and high hopes of modernist architects, the simplistic, supposedly futuristic International Style did not last for centuries. In fact, it had became passé and largely obsolete by the early 1980s. This was partly because many of the people who worked and lived in these buildings found them neither functional nor comfortable. Indeed, critics variously called them stark, bland, sterile, lacking in emotional feeling, and even dehumanizing.

As a result, the last two decades of the twentieth century and first decade of the twenty-first witnessed a new revolution in world architecture. Searching for a convenient label, some

THE CONTROVERSIAL FRANK O. GEHRY

*A*mong the world's greatest architects, Frank O. Gehry is also one of the most controversial. He was born in 1929 in Toronto, Canada, where his grandmother helped him create little cities out of scraps of wood, awakening in him a love of architecture and city planning. When he was seventeen his family moved to California. There he attended the University of Southern California School of Architecture. Later, he studied city planning at the Harvard Graduate School of Design. In time Gehry became famous for his unconventional designs, many of which feature metal surfaces twisted into strange curves and bulging surfaces, often made of shining titanium or other metals. Many regard one of these structures, the Guggenheim Museum in Bilbao, Spain, as his masterpiece. But Gehry has achieved nearly equal fame for his Dancing House in Prague, in the Czech Republic, the oddly twisted contours of which are meant to resemble two dancers. Many people, fellow architects and ordinary people alike, have strongly criticized Gehry's work, saying that it lacks harmony, is not organic enough, or is simply too weird for most people's tastes. However, others call him a visionary. And he is constantly in demand.

The sweeping arcs of the Guggenheim Museum in Bilbao, Spain, reflect the city's lights at dusk.

experts have called it postmodernism. Others prefer the term Second Modernism. And still others emphasize that the movement is highly eclectic, with a diversity of styles; as Neal puts it: "Architecture went in many directions, with no single style dominant," so it "can be described best as Pluralism."[42]

Whatever one chooses to call it, the new trend in monumental architecture has so far been characterized by an effort to make buildings more accessible to people and their needs and comforts. In part, this has entailed a return to aesthetic values to appeal to human emotions. For instance, architects reintroduced color, often bright and gaudy, in both interiors and exteriors; and they added various forms of decoration, including an old standby—Greco-Roman columns. For example, in an addition to the Oberlin College Art Museum (in Oberlin, Ohio), architect Robert Venturi (1925–) filled an open space with an enormous, purely decorative, modified version of a Greek Ionic column. Such touches are more than just attractive and/or at times even humorous or playful. They also give people entering such buildings visual and emotional connections to the greatest cultural achievements of humanity's past.

In addition, many of the newer buildings are designed in free-flowing, complex, highly asymmetrical shapes. A famous example is the Guggenheim Museum (1997) in Bilbao, Spain, designed by Frank O. Gehry (1929–). Made up of a series of flowing, irregularly molded contours, it looks more like a giant sculpture than a traditional building. Similarly, Gehry's Walt Disney Concert Hall (2003) in Los Angeles uses enormous free-flowing curves to achieve a plastic, organic look strikingly different from modernism's plain angular boxes and cubes.

A Bright Future?

Architecture's future is uncertain. But most expert observers think that the present wide variety and mixture of styles will remain the norm for a long time to come. In part, they say, this diversity is driven by the large number of flexible yet durable building materials now available; also, computers, robots, and other technological advances allow architects to experiment with new ideas and translate those ideas into reality on a regular basis.

Moreover, there is a general sense that all of this variety and experimentation is beneficial and will help ensure that architecture has a bright future that produces marvels that can only be guessed at now. A leading twentieth-century American architect, Minoru Yamasaki, stated: "Because we are such a complex civilization, because we do have this incredible amount of material on hand, [and] because of our technology and methods, we have really an immense horizon."[43] These words echo the sentiments of another leading twentieth-century architect, Gio Ponti. "We have a richness of architecture that has never before existed in the world," he said. "My advice is to treasure the future and never look back. The glory of the past was made by others. We have the future, the great unknown, that mystery in front of us. Our architecture must look to the past only to be worthy of the burdens of the past."[44]

Notes

Introduction: A Unique Fusion of Science and Art

1. Vitruvius, *On Architecture*, trans. Frank Granger, vol. 1. Cambridge, MA: Harvard University Press, 2002, p. 7.
2. Vitruvius, *On Architecture*, vol. 1, p. 35.
3. Quoted in H.W. Janson and Anthony F. Janson, *History of Art*. New York: Harry N. Abrams, 1997, p. 630.
4. James Neal, *Architecture: A Visual History*. New York: Sterling, 2001, p. 6.
5. Marvin Trachtenberg and Isabelle Hyman, *Architecture: From Prehistory to Post-Modernism*. New York: Prentice-Hall, 2003, p. 41.
6. Anita Abramovitz, *People and Spaces*. New York: Viking, 1979, pp. 3–4.
7. Neal, *Architecture*, p. 7.
8. Quoted in John Peter, *The Oral History of Modern Architecture: Interviews with the Greatest Architects of the Twentieth Century*. New York: Harry N. Abrams, 1994, p. 128.

Chapter 1: The Earliest Civilizations: The Near East and Europe

9. Trachtenberg and Hyman, *Architecture*, p. 47.
10. Abramovitz, *People and Spaces*, p. 29.
11. Quoted in Desmond Stewart, *The Pyramids and the Sphinx*. New York: Newsweek Book Division, 1971, p. 141.
12. Jeremy B. Rutter et al., "Minoan Architecture: The Palaces," Dartmouth College. http://projectsx.dartmouth.edu/history/bronze_age/lessons/les/12.html.
13. William R. Biers, *The Archaeology of Greece*. Ithaca, NY: Cornell University Press, 1996, p. 29.

Chapter 2: The Earliest Civilizations: Asia and Mesoamerica

14. Neal, *Architecture*, p. 15.
15. Francis D.K. Ching et al., *A Global History of Architecture*. New York: Wiley, 2006, p. 169.
16. Ching, *Global History of Architecture*, p. 383.
17. Quoted in Charles Higham, *The Civilization of Angkor*. Berkeley: University of California Press, 2004, pp. 1–2.
18. Quoted in Chris Scarre, ed., *The Seventy Wonders of the Ancient World*. London: Thames and Hudson, 1999, p. 212.
19. Frederick Hartt, *Art: A History of Painting, Sculpture, and Architecture*.

New York: Prentice-Hall, 2003, p. 59.

Chapter 3: The Classical Tradition: Ancient Greece and Rome

20. Neal, *Architecture*, p. 11.
21. Quoted in Peter Green, *The Parthenon*. New York: Newsweek, 1973, p. 155.
22. Abramovitz, *People and Spaces*, p. 54.
23. Mortimer Wheeler, *Roman Art and Architecture*. London: Thames and Hudson, 1985, p. 9.

Chapter 4: Castles and Cathedrals: The Medieval Era

24. Sidney Toy, *Castles: Their Construction and History*. New York: Dover, 1985, p. xiii.
25. Quoted in Janson and Janson, *History of Art*, p. 383.
26. Quoted in Leon Bernard and Theodore B. Hodges, eds., *Readings in European History*. New York: Macmillan, 1961, p. 169.
27. Michael Raeburn, *Architecture of the World*. New York: Galahad, 1975, p. 34.
28. Janson and Janson, *History of Art*, p. 322.
29. L. Sprague de Camp, *The Ancient Engineers*. New York: Barnes and Noble, 1993, p. 359.

Chapter 5: The Age of Domes: Europe's Renaissance

30. Quoted in Janson and Janson, *History of Art*, p. 635.

31. Raeburn, *Architecture of the World*, p. 56.
32. Quoted in Janson and Janson, *History of Art*, p. 630.
33. Abramovitz, *People and Spaces*, p. 135.
34. Janson and Janson, *History of Art*, pp. 419–20.
35. Hartt, *Art*, p. 631.

Chapter 6: Idealizing the Past: The Early Modern Period

36. Abramovitz, *People and Spaces*, p. 149.
37. Janson and Janson, *History of Art*, p. 560.
38. Neal, *Architecture*, p. 23.
39. Quoted in Saul K. Padover, ed., *Thomas Jefferson and the National Capital*, letter dated April 10, 1791. Washington, DC: U.S. Government Printing Office, 1946, p. 59.

Chapter 7: New Innovations: The Twentieth Century and Beyond

40. Mario Salvadori, *Why Buildings Stand Up: The Strength of Architecture*. New York: Norton, 1990, pp. 66–67.
41. Trachtenberg and Hyman, *Architecture*, p. 553.
42. Neal, *Architecture*, p. 32.
43. Quoted in Peter, *Oral History of Modern Architecture*, p. 286.
44. Quoted in Peter, *Oral History of Modern Architecture*, p. 289.

Glossary

acropolis: In a Greek city-state, a central hill used for defensive and religious purposes. The most famous example is the Acropolis in Athens.

aesthetic: Relating to emotions, feelings, and/or artistic impulses.

amphitheater: A wooden or stone structure, usually oval-shaped and open at the top, in which the ancient Romans staged public games and shows.

archaeologists: Experts who dig up and study past civilizations.

bailey: In medieval Europe, a courtyard, usually enclosed by a defensive wall.

balustrade: An architectural decoration consisting of a row of repeating posts (balusters) topped by a railing.

bronze: A metal alloy made by mixing copper and tin.

capital: The topmost section of a column.

cella: The main room of a Greek temple.

circus: A long wooden or stone structure in which the ancient Romans staged horse and chariot races.

coffering: Sunken or recessed areas of wooden or stone panels, most often in ceilings.

colonnade: A row of columns.

corbeling: A technique of making roofs (or ceilings) in which layers of stone are stacked so that each layer slightly overhangs the one below it.

crenellation: The notched effect in the battlements of forts, castles, and other ancient and medieval structures.

cromlech: A circular structure composed of megalithic stones, the most famous example being Stonehenge in southern England.

drawbridge: A movable wooden platform spanning a moat in front of a castle's main gate.

euripus (or *spina*): The long, narrow, highly ornamented barrier running down the middle of a Roman racetrack.

frieze: A decorative painted or sculpted band running horizontally along a temple's entablature.

hall: The principal chamber in the living quarters of a medieval castle or house.

hypostyle hall: A large interior chamber whose roof is held up by numerous columns evenly distributed across the room.

mastaba: A low, rectangular tomb made of stone or mud bricks.

master mason: In medieval times, a combination of architect, building contractor, and general overseer.

megalithic: Made up of huge stones.

metope: In a Doric entablature, a rectangular panel flanked by triglyphs and bearing a painting or sculpted relief.

motte: In medieval Europe, an earthen mound on which early castles were built.

order: An architectural style, usually identified by the main features of its columns. Columns in the Doric order have no decorative bases, and their capitals are topped by plain rectangular slabs. Columns in the Ionic order do have decorative bases, and their capitals are topped by ornamental scrolls.

pediment: A triangular gable at the top of the front or back of a Greek-style temple.

pilaster: An architectural decoration consisting of a partial or flattened column that projects only slightly from a wall.

portcullis: A heavy grated door, usually of oak shod with iron, that raised and lowered vertically in a castle's main gateway.

post and lintel: The basic architectural arrangement of a vertical support (the post) topped by a horizontal beam (the lintel).

pylon: A large, flat-topped ceremonial gateway that became a common feature of Egyptian temples.

reliefs (or bas-reliefs): Sculpted images or scenes in which the figures and/or objects depicted are raised from but still attached to a flat surface.

shell keep: A small castle composed of a single circular wall enclosing an inner courtyard, usually built atop a hill.

shikhara: The pagoda-like tower of a Hindu temple.

stupa: In India and other Far Eastern lands, a hemispheric mound or domelike structure that became a basic architectural motif of Buddhist and Hindu temples.

tensile strength: The amount of stress a material can endure before it breaks.

vedka: In Far Eastern architecture, a balustrade running around the perimeter or dome of a temple.

volute: An elegant spiral scroll at the top of an Ionic capital.

ziggurat: In ancient Mesopotamia, a large sacred mound on the summit of which rested a temple or shrine.

For Further Reading

Books

Enrico Annosica et al., *Art: A World History*. London: Dorling Kindersley, 1998. One of the best general overviews of art history available.

Francis D.K. Ching et al., *A Global History of Architecture*. New York: Wiley, 2006. A large and comprehensive overview of architecture through the ages in all parts of the world. Highly recommended.

Alan Colquhoun, *Modern Architecture*. New York: Oxford University Press, 2002. A well-illustrated, well-written examination of the subject.

H.W. Janson and Anthony F. Janson, *History of Art*. New York: Harry N. Abrams, 1997. A major study of art history and achievement. Contains a great deal about the evolution of architecture, including numerous excellent photos of key structures.

H.W. Kauffman et al., *The Medieval Fortress: Castles, Forts, and Walled Cities of the Middle Ages*. New York: Da Capo, 2004. An excellent overview of medieval architecture and building techniques, along with lots of information about how medieval structures were used.

Marian Moffett et al., *A World History of Architecture*. New York: McGraw-Hill, 2003. Similar in aim and scope to Ching's book (see above). Also highly recommended.

Don Nardo, *Great Structures of Ancient Egypt*. San Diego: Lucent, 2005. A clearly written overview of ancient Egyptian architecture, structures, and building methods.

———, *Greek Temples*. New York: Franklin Watts, 2002. Discusses the development of Greek temple architecture and highlights the Parthenon and other notable Greek structures.

Web Sites

The Megalithic Temples of Malta (www. web.infinito.it/utenti/m/malta_mega_te mples). This enlightening examination of some of the earliest examples of stone architecture in the world is provided by the Archaeology on the Net Web Ring.

Michelangelo Buonarroti (www.michel angelo.com/buonarroti.html). The home page of an excellent series of Web sites devoted to the life and works of one of the greatest architects who ever lived. Contains many stunning photos of his buildings, sculptures, and paintings.

The Pantheon (www.greatbuildings.com/ buildings/Pantheon.html). This site, part of the online series GreatBuildings.com, provides loads of information about one of ancient Rome's greatest architectural achievements, along with numerous color photos of the Pantheon. Click on the link for the GreatBuildings home page to explore other famous buildings from around the world.

Skyscrapers Webography (www.pbs.org/wgbh/buildingbig/skyscraper/webography.html). A collection of links to useful, informative sites about well-known skyscrapers around the world.

Index

role in architecture, 9–10
Temples
  Egyptian, 20
  of Greece, 39–44
  Hindu, 32–35
  Mesopotamian, 18–19
Teotihuacán (Mexico), 37
Theater of Dionysus, 45
Traditionalism, 93–94

V
Van Alen, William, 94
Van der Rohe, Ludwig Mies, 97
Vasari, Giorgio, 76
Vault, Roman, 48, 50
Venturi, Robert, 99

Vitruvius (Roman architect), 9–10
Vooswars, 48

W
Walt Disney Concert Hall (Los Angeles),
  100
Waterhouse, Alfred, 88
William of Sens, 60
Woolworth Building (New York City), 93
Wright, Frank Lloyd, 13, 94–96, 97

Y
Yamasaki, Minoru, 100

Z
Ziggurats, 18–19

Picture Credits

Cover: Reproduced by permission of Gstar
© Adam Woolfitt/CORBIS, 30, 62, 78
© Andrew Watson/Alamy, 99
© Archivo Iconografico, S.A./CORBIS, 67
The Art Archive/Gianni Dagli Orti, 36, 74
Bildarchiv Preussischer Kulturbesitz/Art
    Resource, NY, 40
© Bob Krist/CORBIS, 23, 34
Brand X Pictures/JupiterImages, 61 (main)
© Colin Dixon/Arcaid/CORBIS, 44
Creatas Images/JupiterImages, 91
© CuboImages srl/Alamy, 69
© Dean Conger/CORBIS, 19
© Douglas Pearson/CORBIS, 47
© Elio Ciol/CORBIS, 83
Erich Lessing/Art Resource, NY, 80
© Ethel Davies/Robert Harding World
    Imagery/CORBIS, 86
© George Hammerstein/Solus-Veer/
    CORBIS, 93 (inset)
Getty Images, 88
© Graham Bell/Alamy, 54
© Images&Stories/Alamy, 56
© Israel images/Alamy, 16
© John Van Hasselt/CORBIS SYGMA, 59
© Leonard de Selva/CORBIS, 55

© M. Dillon/CORBIS, 15
© Maximilian Weinzierl/Alamy, 24
© North Wind Picture Archives/Alamy, 42
© Origlia Franco/CORBIS SYGMA, 79
© Patrick Ward/CORBIS, 53
Pixland/JupiterImages, 75
© Richard A. Cooke/CORBIS, 96
© Richard T. Nowitz/CORBIS, 32
Robert Harding Picture Library
    Ltd/Alamy, 9
Robert Preston/Alamy, 11
© Ron Sachs/CNP/CORBIS, 65
The Step Pyramid of King Djoser, c. 2630–
    2611 B.C. (photo), Egyptian, 3rd
    Dynasty (2700-2620 B.C.)/Saqqara,
    Egypt/The Bridgeman Art Library
    International, 21
© Rudy Sulgan/CORBIS, 93 (main)
© Svenja-Foto/zefa/CORBIS, 61 (inset)
© Tibor Bognar/Alamy, 28
Time Life Pictures/Getty Images, 49
View of the Nave, 1425-46 (photo),
    Brunelleschi, Filippo (1377-1446)/San
    Lorenzo, Lorenzo, Florence, Italy/
    The Bridgeman Art Library
    International , 71

About the Author

Historian and literary scholar Don Nardo is best known for his books for young people about the ancient world, including numerous volumes on the history and culture of ancient Mesopotamia, Egypt, Greece, and Rome. He has also written many books about art and literature, among them a history of sculpture and literary companions to the works of Homer, Sophocles, Euripides, Chaucer, Shakespeare, and Dickens. Nardo lives with his wife, Christine, in Massachusetts.